my Multiple Sclerosis story

attitude
is everything

Conor Devine

This is the story of one man's incredible journey back to health and fulfillment. Conor shares, very intimately, how he implemented a three-point plan to beat multiple sclerosis.

ACKNOWLEDGEMENTS

Whenever you are faced with adversity of any kind, it can be extremely difficult to come through the many challenges that lie in front of you if you are left to your own devices. I have been very fortunate to have a select number of people who were there for me when I was on the floor, and who gave me the encouragement and support I needed to get my act together, fight the condition, and climb my mountain. Without this support, I may not be where I am today, so I would now like to take this opportunity to thank those people who helped me through my toughest days.

My mum and dad, thank you for never giving up on me and for praying for me continuously to get better and get the strength to fight my way through my battles; to my sister Ciara, who has been my guardian angel since I was a little boy playing in the garden, and has always been there to help and advise me; to Colm and Barry for being great friends and brothers and being understanding, when I was getting things fairly difficult; to Denis, Loretta, and family for putting up with me and giving me support throughout my challenges; and to my previous employer, Btw Shiells, thank you for all your support at a time when I was really struggling. This kept me going and was a huge help to me in my time of need.

To Dr. Mike and the medical team at Mauritius—thank you for keeping me calm and taking good care of me when the virus first set in. To my GP, Dr. Cullen, thank you for being there for me when I needed a chat, supporting me through all my tough times, and going the extra mile when I needed your care and expertise. I thank my neurologist, Dr. Watt, for looking after me, giving me fantastic advice, and putting up with all my questions in the early days.

To my great friend James, thanks for all the support over the past few years. "A friend is someone who helps you up when you're down, and if they can't, they lie down beside you and listen." James you are that guy—so, thank you.

To Bertie for believing in me and encouraging me to keep pushing the bar a little higher every day and accept that dreamers can in fact move mountains.

To Kate, my best friend and rock, who has seen me at my very lowest, thanks for putting up with me all these years and continuing to show me your love, affection, and support. You believed that I could get here by encouraging me to pursue my dreams. I will be forever grateful to you for this, and I love you dearly.

Fall down seven times; get up eight times
—— Chinese proverb

TABLE OF CONTENTS

WHAT IS MULTIPLE SCLEROSIS?

Multiple sclerosis (abbreviated to MS) is an inflammatory disease in which the fatty myelin sheaths around the axons of the brain and spinal cord are damaged, leading to demyelination and scarring, as well as a broad spectrum of signs and symptoms. Disease onset usually occurs in young adults, and it is more common in women.

MS affects the ability of nerve cells in the brain and spinal cord to communicate with each other effectively. This causes a range of uncomfortable symptoms for the person with the condition.

Almost any neurological symptom can appear with the disease, and it often progresses to physical and cognitive disability. MS takes several forms, with new symptoms occurring either in discrete attacks (relapsing forms) or slowly accumulating over time (progressive forms). Between attacks, symptoms may go away completely, but permanent neurological problems often occur—especially as the disease advances.

There is currently no known cure for multiple sclerosis. Treatments attempt to return function after an attack, prevent new attacks, and prevent disability. MS medications can slow the onset of the disease, and there are a number of treatments available known as disease modifying drugs.

<u>There are 4 types of MS, namely;</u>

1. Benign MS

2. Relapsing Remitting

3. Secondary Progressive

4. Primary Progressive

There are an estimated twelve thousand people in Ireland (North and South) affected with MS, one hundred thousand in the UK, and over 2.5 million people worldwide. My own view is that this figure could be a lot higher as many may not be officially diagnosed.

There are many symptoms of multiple sclerosis, over fifty in total. A person with MS can suffer almost any neurological symptom or sign, including changes in sensation, such as loss of sensitivity or tingling, pricking or numbness, muscle weakness, muscle spasms, or difficulty in moving; difficulties with coordination and balance; problems in speech or swallowing, visual problems, fatigue, acute or chronic pain, and bladder and bowel difficulties. Cognitive impairment of varying degrees and emotional symptoms of depression or unstable mood are also common. Lhermitte's sign, an electrical sensation that runs down the back when bending the neck, is a particular characteristic of MS although not specific. I suffered from this symptom in the early days after diagnosis and it is very distressing.

Symptoms of MS usually appear in episodic acute periods of worsening (called relapses, exacerbations, bouts, attacks, or "flare-ups"), in a gradually progressive deterioration of neurologic function, or in a combination of both. Multiple sclerosis relapses are often unpredictable, occurring without warning and without obvious inciting factors with a rate rarely above one and a half per year. Some attacks, however, are preceded by common triggers. Relapses tend to occur more frequently during spring and summer. Viral infections such as the common cold, influenza, or gastroenteritis increase the risk of relapse. Stress may also trigger an attack. Pregnancy affects the susceptibility to relapse, with a lower relapse rate at each trimester of gestation.

Most likely, MS occurs as a result of some combination of genetic, environmental, and infectious factors.

It does not sound like much fun, does it? That is one way of looking at it.

PROLOGUE

It was the night before one of the happiest days of my life. I was out having a few drinks with my friends and family celebrating the fact that the following day I was getting married to my childhood sweetheart, Kate Loughrey. Life could not get much better. I had a good job, I was very fit and healthy, and I was about to start the next very exciting chapter of my life. Over the course of the next two weeks, my dreams were shattered as I got a virus that resulted in me being diagnosed with a neurological condition called multiple sclerosis.

Three years into my illness and at the grand old age of thirty-one years old, I felt as though all was lost. I had let this bastard of a thing called multiple sclerosis take over everything, ruin my life, and kill all of my dreams. My symptoms were extremely difficult, I was in a dark hole, and I had accepted that all was lost. I was going to be sick for the rest of my life and it was likely that I would end up in a wheelchair being pushed around by my beautiful wife. I was in a constant state of pity: feeling sorry for myself, feeling sorry for my wife and family, feeling useless, and feeling as though I was a hindrance to everyone.

Then something peculiar happened. One day I decided that I was going to take control of the situation. I decided that I was going to take control of my brain, take control of my MS, and take control of my life. Three years on, and my life has completely changed for the good. I am a new person with more drive than five of the old me's put together. I have turned things around and have an unrivalled zest for life.

If someone had said to me shortly after my diagnosis that I would have turned my life around, beat MS and had written a book to share my story with the world, I would have said they were crazy. However, I started thinking about writing this book twelve months ago as I got an overwhelming feeling of responsibility that I needed to share my story with others. After speaking to a few people over a period of time, it became very clear to me that my story was inspiring some people to fight back against their illness and giving others some hope to fight on in whatever challenges they faced in their lives.

I now know I can help some people believe that there is hope and light at the end of the tunnel, and this is an incredible feeling. I want to put on record that I am no different or no better a person than anyone else who is fighting MS, or any other form of illness for that matter, apart from a few ingredients. With these ingredients, I believe that I am testament that you too can turn your life around and start reversing your symptoms and live life to the full.

Many warriors out there—many great people— do wonderful things day in and day out, and they never get to share their stories for different reasons. I am very fortunate that I am in a position where I can do this, and I truly believe that attitude is everything, and if you apply the right attitude to whatever mountain you are climbing in your life, you will conquer. Illness and the range of other problems life can throw at you can cause a lot of destruction and difficulties. Life can mess with your brain, mess with your hopes and dreams, and drive you to the brink of self-destruction. MS can distort your body, and in some cases, ruin your life; however, for me it will never take my mind, and of that, I am certain.

It has been a journey in itself writing this short book, and I feel a great sense of pride that through my story I know others will benefit and start to believe in themselves. If one person in the world is inspired by my story and starts to fight back, this will have been a truly successful exercise. Life is not an audition; you are the star of your own movie, and unfortunately, there are no dress rehearsals. So start to fight back, fight disease, fight illness, design your life around your goals, and remember that if you have and apply the right attitude, believe me—anything is possible.

The other important message I would like to get out via my book is that writing about MS is quite difficult as the symptoms of the condition vary from person to person. What is true for one may not be true for another. While I believe it is great to applaud someone for running a marathon or climbing a mountain, I also believe it is equally right to applaud someone who takes a few steps every day after a bad episode or who endures chronic symptoms with stoicism and grace. The important common denominator in everyone who is winning the battle against illness or whatever challenges they may have is that they have developed the right attitude to get them through each day.

A wise man said to me once that huge mountains are removed stone by stone—you just have to keep going and you will get there!

I hope you enjoy my story.

CHAPTER 1   MAURITIUS

My eyes opened, and I glanced at the clock to see that it was 8.30 a.m. I was lying beside my new beautiful wife in a luxurious hotel in Mauritius, five thousand miles from home. I had married Kate a few days previous on Saturday, 18 August 2006, and I was the happiest man in the world.

The last three months had been the most exciting chapters in my life to date. Both Kate and I had gone through all the details of the wedding with a fine-toothed comb and it was just hitting me as I lay in bed how perfect everything had turned out to be—absolutely fantastic. The wedding day was terrific from the service right through to the reception, and to be completely honest, it could not have turned out any better. We held the reception in Harvey's Point in Donegal, which really is one of Ireland's best-kept secrets. The standout memory had to be my dad, one of the most talented musicians I have ever witnessed, playing the hotel piano into the wee small hours, keeping everyone in song and spirit. It is one of my favorite memories of all time.

I jumped out of bed and ran over to the window to check the view from our deluxe honeymoon suite. I pulled the curtains and the view was absolutely superb. The pool was just a few feet away, and there was a private beach close by leading to the Indian Ocean.

I was feeling quite tired, obviously from all the exertion of the past two weeks, but generally I was in great form and so looking forward to the next ten days with Kate to completely chill out.

"Kate, I am going to nip down to the beach for twenty minutes, so I'll be back soon!" I shouted, not sure, whether she heard me, as she seemed out cold, obviously exhausted from the last few days. One of the things I love to do when on holiday is get into the water first thing in the morning. Water is fantastic and really freshens you up—putting you in good form for the day ahead. Therefore, off I went for my early morning dip with the beautiful thoughts of how I was going to spend the next ten days with Kate.

I came back up to the room, and Kate was up and unpacking the cases and getting ready to head out to the pool. One of the things we really enjoy doing together is going on holiday and just relaxing in the sun. It was a time for relaxation, and the fact that this was our honeymoon made everything extra special.

Around mid-day, we were starting to feel a little peckish, so we decided to make our way to a restaurant by the sea for some lunch. The hotel was spectacular and beautifully positioned in the northern part of the island. The views from the open-air restaurant over the ocean were exquisite, and there was a good atmosphere at the resort with what seemed like lots of honeymooners all appearing very lovey dovey, so we fit in just fine. Kate looked great and seemed very relaxed, and although I was feeling quite worn out and a little tired to be honest, ever the warrior, I did not pass any remarks.

We placed our order with our waiter, and then something very strange happened. A weird sensation of pins and needles started to take over my right hand. It came on me very quickly, and initially, I did not say anything to Kate as I was hoping it would go away. However, over the next few minutes, the pins and needles started to move up my arm to my elbow, and it was at this point that I started to get concerned.

I excused myself and went to the bathroom to check my complexion and splash some water on my face. I went over to the wash-hand basin and gazed in the mirror, and to my surprise, I looked fine. I had color in my face, so what the hell was going on. I returned to my seat completely bemused with what had just happened but hoping that it would disappear immediately so I could get on with enjoying my lunch. However, after a few minutes, the weird sensations returned, Kate sensed that I was not feeling very good. She knew from my tone and expressions that something was up, so I tried to explain to her that my right arm was now completely numb and tingling for no apparent reason.

Kate was immediately concerned, and it was fair to assume at this stage that I was petrified. Although I was in no physical pain, I was starting to get very anxious and was feeling vulnerable with the one question repeating itself in my mind: *What the hell is happening to me?* My appetite disappeared, and we decided to bring our first honeymoon lunch date to a swift conclusion, so we asked the restaurant manager to deliver Kate's food to the room as I wanted to go back to bed to see if resting would help me in any way.

Over the course of the next few hours, I lay in bed and the numbness remained in my right arm. I was trying to understand what was going on, but could not work out what the problem was. I had never experienced anything like this before in my life, and it just did not make any sense to me at all.

The remainder of the day consisted of me lying on bed sipping water and trying to eat some food to pass the time; however, I could not relax at all due to the problem in my arm. My appetite was non-existent. Kate was supportive but probably felt quite helpless, and I would say fairly peeved with what was going on. All I could think was that I was on my honeymoon, supposed to be having the time of my life, and what happens? I get sick. It was all too unbelievable!

The day passed very slowly and I tried to do some reading to take my mind off the weird sensations that were coming and going throughout my body. Around 1:00 a.m., as I was drifting in and out of consciousness completely exhausted, an electric shock-like sensation, which felt like someone had just turned a Bunsen burner on me, moved up my right arm. I nearly fell out of bed with panic, and for the first time, I was in some pain for a few seconds. I turned on the light and told Kate that maybe I should go to the hospital, as I did not feel well at all and I was very worried.

As my arm settled for a few moments, I also settled slightly; however, something strange was starting to happen. The sensation of pins and needles seemed like it was progressing up my right arm towards my shoulder. I was starting to get very frightened now, as it was quite unbelievable what was happening to my body. I looked at the clock and saw that it was 2:15 a.m.; I was sweating with fear and worry. The only way I can describe what was happening is if you can imagine being bitten by a snake, and now you are feeling the venom moving up your arm. To clear things up, I have never been bitten by a snake in my life but I have worked with a few over the years.

When the tingling progressed to the bottom of my head, I jumped out of bed, got dressed, and both of us ran to the reception desk and asked to be taken to the hospital immediately. The night porter ordered a cab, which arrived a short time later. We both jumped into the cab, and the driver could not speak a word of English, which did not really matter at that point, as I was not looking to ask him what type of day he was having. His brief was very clear—to get me to the hospital in super quick time, and no messing about!

We left the complex and went in what I thought had better be in the direction of the hospital along some of the worst roads I had ever travelled on in my entire life. The first ten miles of the car journey was on some form of dirt track through sugar cane fields that lined either side and looked as if we were going deeper into a jungle, as opposed to going in the direction of the island's hospital. The pins and needles sensations were travelling now and seemed to be making their way to the left side of my body.

I am being completely honest when I say this now, but for the first time since the incident began eighteen hours earlier, I was starting to fear for my life. I had no idea what was going on with my body, but whatever it was, I knew it was not good. One thing I am not is stupid, and I knew full well that this was not one-bit normal. My whole life was flashing before me, and all of this on honeymoon with my wife in the back seat of an old Volvo taxi, over 20 years old, in the middle of nowhere at 3:00 a.m. in the morning. All I could think was, *What the hell is going on? And why the hell is it happening to me?*

After about forty-five minutes, which felt like three days, I saw a sign on the road, which I recognized as that for a hospital. Thank God, I was now close by, where at least I would be safe instead of sitting in the hotel room twiddling my thumbs. Kate spent most of the journey trying to reassure me that things would be fine, but despite her best intentions, it was not working. I was getting further into a state of fear and anxiety. Since the moment I stepped foot into the cab, I had recited the Hail Mary over and over again, asking God to look after me and help me pull through whatever was going on with me. I always had a deep enough faith and at this point in time I really did need the boss-man upstairs to pull me out of this hole.

The taxi slowed down and indicated a right turn, and I could see that we had arrived at the hospital. It seemed more like a health centre than a hospital, but then again, we were in Mauritius and not Belfast. At that point, I did not care, as long as the doctors and medical team were good. I needed urgent medical attention, so just getting out of the taxi was all that was going through my mind.

The last time I felt like I was going to die was when I was holidaying with my family in the former Yugoslavia when we got caught up in a series of earth tremors (mini earthquakes). Not a nice feeling, and I was only thirteen years old; however, fast forward fifteen years and the feeling that I was close to death returned to me, and I am telling you right now, it is not a nice experience.

Kate and I walked into the hospital, and right away we were greeted by two very friendly Mauritian nurses who told me that Dr. Mike would be with me very soon. As we sat in the waiting room in the middle of the night, Kate kept telling me things would be fine, but I just could not see that being the case. I was starting to get very upset with the occurrences of the past twenty-four hours, and I just could not accept what was happening. The nurse handed me a small book, which had been signed by previous patients of the hospital, all stating how pleased they were with the standard of medical attention they had experienced at the hospital at the hands of this Dr. Mike. That was all very good; however, not much good to a man who was hours from death, unless I was sorted out very soon; so, thanks for the book, but it was not really what I needed right now.

After about ten minutes, a man came over to me and introduced himself as Dr. Mike. My first impressions were good. He was slightly taller than me, a little tubby in appearance, had a smiley face, and he did look as if he knew what he was doing. He spoke with good authority, had excellent English, and assured me that I would be fine, but that I needed to stay calm. For a few split seconds, he did put my mind at ease, and I thought that maybe I was going to be okay. He went on to ask me what the problem was, so I explained to him my symptoms and he immediately started to carry out a range of tests while going through a list of questions.

The questions and examinations went on for an hour or more and I was just happy now that I was in the hands of someone who seemed to know what he was talking about. When that was completed, he advised me that I needed an MRI scan. I had experienced scans before as a result of football injuries on my knees and ankles; however, this time he explained that an MRI was required to have a look at my brain. I did not know a lot about MRI scans, but I did know that what was happening to me must be serious if I needed to get a brain scan.

As I walked down the corridor towards the MRI unit, I got a little upset and felt even more vulnerable. My new wife was in reception, it was 5:00 a.m. in the morning, I was on my honeymoon, and so far away from my family—it just all seemed so unfair.

The scan itself is quite a daunting experience, as you are literally put in a cylinder, your head in a cask, and told not to move for forty-five minutes.

After the scan, I was shown to my room where Kate was waiting for me. The nurse told me that Dr. Mike wanted me to stay in hospital for a day or two, and that if I needed something, all I had to do was ask. What I really wanted was for whatever was going on in my body to go away so that I could get back to my hotel and enjoy the rest of my honeymoon. As I lay there, I knew that was just not going to happen anytime soon. The nurse left the room and Kate lay down beside me. Feelings of guilt were starting to set in; it felt as if I had ruined everything. I knew Kate was absolutely exhausted and was as sick with worry as was I, but there was nothing each of us could do but hope and pray that everything was going to be okay.

Kate had been fantastic throughout the past twenty-four hours, and that did not surprise me. Over the previous ten years, I had grown to understand that although small in stature, Kate was an incredibly strong, compassionate woman with a massive heart, and was an excellent support mechanism to me whenever I really needed her. I tried to introduce a little humour into the situation by reminding her of the vows she had made a few days earlier: "In sickness and in health." I was really testing the resolve in the first few days of marriage, eh? We both smiled and hugged each other and tried to get some rest. I couldn't sleep, though, as all I could think about was Kate, my mum and dad at home, my brothers and sister, my career, and my marriage; everything seemed completely doomed, and every time I tried to close my eyes, it all flashed in front of me. What was supposed to be the greatest experience in my life was turning into a complete nightmare—worse than that—a disaster that I may never escape. I was lying in a bloody hospital thousands of miles from home and possibly about to die. Why me? Why the hell me?

————————

Over the course of the next few hours, my symptoms continued, and it felt at times that my entire body was on fire. Pins and needles everywhere, and throw in some sort of electrical shock feeling every now and then, and you can imagine the crack was mighty – Not!

After a few hours and a number of failed attempts to get some rest, Dr. Mike walked into my room and told me that all my tests came back clear. "What do you mean clear? You must be joking; I know myself, and I am not well," I said with anger in my voice. In a funny way, I was somewhat disappointed; I knew something was wrong and just wanted the doctor to confirm, if nothing else, for my sanity. He told me that initially he thought I might have had a small stroke; however, as I was quite young and fit, and after tests including the MRI scan, he had determined that was not the case.

The one thing he did mention was that he saw from the scans a kink in my neck and a little inflammation around that area. I put that down to my flight over on the plane, possibly with my neck in the same place for a number of hours. He said that with all the running around in the past two weeks with the marriage and travel, all the stress and anxiety could be the cause for the pins and needles, and in his opinion, things should settle in a day or two. He was of the opinion I had contracted some sort of virus that had got into my immune system and was the cause of the problems, but he expected it to resolve itself in time. *Who does he think he is?* I thought. *I don't do stress, and I don't need some doctor telling me that I am stressed out—absolute bollocks.*

One thing I did agree with reluctantly was that Dr. Mike thought I should stay in the hospital for a day or two so that they could keep an eye on me. I knew that the hospital was the best place for me, but I was so sorry for Kate due to the fact that she would be on her own at the resort, which was not ideal at all. However, she told me it was no problem, and she made her way back to the hotel and left me alone in the hospital. I did my best to relax and tried to get a couple of hours' rest, but my brain was unable to relax.

Throughout the next few days, my symptoms remained the same. Dr. Mike was excellent to be fair to him and kept trying to give me some confidence by telling me that everything was going to be okay. After the initial twenty-four hours in hospital, I had a chance to speak with my mum and dad on the phone to keep them updated on what was going on. I think at this stage, everyone at home had heard that I had taken unwell on honeymoon. They were all very concerned. My mum just kept saying that God would look after us and she was praying very hard for me.

My mum and dad brought us up as practicing Catholics. We always went to Mass, and from a young age, my parents had always encouraged us to believe in God and that it was important to have a strong faith. I was very fortunate that this deep faith in God was present in me when I found myself in this desperate situation, as I definitely needed some help from the man upstairs, but I would have been a lot happier if he had hurried up!

I returned to the resort after my short spell in hospital and Kate was delighted to see me back with her; however, in truth, I was no better, and to be honest, the whole honeymoon was now more or less ruined. After speaking with Kate and my parents on the phone, we all agreed that we should return home immediately and get a second medical opinion as soon as possible. Over the next twenty-four hours, we tried to get the next available flight out of Mauritius to London, but there were no flights available, so we agreed reluctantly that there was nothing we could do just yet. We may as well enjoy what time we had left. After all, I did get the all clear and was in no immediate danger, according to Dr. Mike. I just didn't think so somehow. I didn't give a damn what the doctor said; I knew there was something badly wrong with me—my body was doing all sorts of weird things, and I didn't need a doctor to tell me I was grand when I knew full well I was very ill.

Over the remainder of the honeymoon, my symptoms remained and comprised pins and needles all over my body, pressure in my head, balance problems, and electrical shocks running intermittently throughout my body. I felt awful and was convinced something bad was happening. Dr. Mike seemed like a great bloke, but he must have got this one wrong as I felt like shit every day and wasn't getting any better. The sense of guilt was increasing day by day. Even though Kate was putting on a brave face about things, I knew she was devastated by what was happening. We spent so much time, energy, and money planning our wedding and honeymoon and were looking forward to the first few years in marriage, and then this happens—I get sick. What a complete disaster, and it just seemed so unfair.

Ever the trooper, I tried to act as normal as possible for the last few days, and we went for meals in the evening and sunbathed during the day. The truth of the matter is that I was petrified with what was going on in my body and hadn't a clue as to what the causes were. I knew something bad had happened but just couldn't work out what it was. I really just wanted to get back to Belfast as quickly as possible, as I felt I needed a second opinion, and as the days went on, my confidence waned in Dr. Mike and his team's prognosis.

Your attitude, not your aptitude, will determine your altitude.
— ZIG ZIGLAR

CHAPTER 2   ACCIDENT AND EMERGENCY

We arrived back in Belfast the following week, and to be honest, my symptoms remained the same and I sank deeper into a cycle of depression with the onset of my illness. I was getting waves of strange symptoms every day, and my brain was in overdrive trying to work out what was going on. I was also desperately trying to figure out how I was going to manage everything going forward. One of my first tasks when I arrived home was to call my employers to let them know that I had taken ill on honeymoon and that I wouldn't be in for a day or two.

I work in the property industry and had qualified as a chartered surveyor twelve months previous. I was extremely ambitious, very hard working and so looking forward to a great career in business and property. This bout of sickness was getting in my way, and I really struggled to get my head around this part, as I was desperate to get back to work and push on with my career. I loved my work, and the onset of this sickness was a hammer blow from a career perspective.

With the way I was feeling over the last couple of weeks, I was starting to believe that my career was over. Thankfully, my employer extremely understood, and told me to take whatever time off I needed. That was very important to me, and I will be forever grateful for their support at that time. It went some small way to making things a little better. I truly believed at that stage that I would be off work for a week or two and be back at the desk once this thing, whatever it was, had passed.

The next thing I had to do was make an appointment with my GP, get a second opinion, and get myself sorted out once and for all. My GP was a great guy, and I really respected him from a medical and personal point of view. He told me immediately that due to my symptoms he needed to refer me to a neurologist as soon as possible and that he would send a fax to the independent clinic in Belfast immediately. He was very concerned about my condition and my state of mind, and he thought it was important to act quickly on this.

So I was being sent to a neurologist; I had heard the term before but I didn't really know what these guys specialized in. Thankfully, I got an appointment scheduled for the following week with Dr. Watt in Belfast, and couldn't wait to go and see if I could get any clarification as to what the hell was happening to me.

My main symptoms at this stage were pins and needles all over my body, severe balance problems, and shooting nerve pain in my legs and chest region. I had also developed a chronic stress-like pressure in my head, and generally, I felt very unwell every day. To be honest, it felt as if I was slowly dying. Physically I still looked fine, possibly a little gaunt, and if you had of met me at that time, you would have thought I was as healthy as the next man; however, internally I felt as if a bolt of lightning had struck my body, and I was not well at all.

That weekend Ireland was playing Cyprus in Dublin and I was sitting in the living room trying my best to relax, sipping a pint of Guinness, and looking forward to watching the game. I still felt like crap and was filled with anxiety, as I believed one hundred percent that there was something seriously wrong with me. I was convinced there was no way you could feel this bad and not be very ill. Since I'd got home, I'd had access to the computer twenty-four hours a day, and I'd say for eighteen of those hours I was researching medical conditions that involved my symptoms.

On hindsight, this is not a very clever thing to do; however, it gave me some satisfaction at that time. Throughout these early days, I had myself diagnosed with Cancer, Transfer Myelitis, and Motor Neuron Disease to name a few, and Google became my new best friend. The big downside to the Internet is that if you are sick and you type in your symptoms, quite a number of conditions will come up, and it can be very worrying and an extremely unhelpful exercise.

As I was sitting watching the Ireland match, a tingling sensation started in my right hand yet again for no apparent reason. It was very similar to what happened in Mauritius. *Here we go again,* I thought, but this time I completely freaked out and was convinced that I was hours from death. I went into deep shock, as the tingling got stronger. I started to panic straight away. I was convinced something bad was happening to me. It really was a terrible feeling, and I would not want anyone else to experience it.

I shouted to Kate that I wanted to go to hospital immediately, so we drove at top speed like two maniacs, racing through red lights with the hazard lights on to the Belfast City Hospital. If the police had of spotted us en route, there would have been no doubt at all that we would have been pulled over for reckless driving. However, with the way I was feeling, we wouldn't have pulled over anyway as I was in hysterics. My breathing was irregular and I was sweating heavily. I felt as if my chest was about to explode into millions of pieces, and my mental state was very poor. My arm was now almost completely numb and I was praying to God to spare me as I was much too young to die—even if it was just until I got to the hospital where I would get some medical attention, which might give me a chance. Kate was quiet and scared and probably didn't know what was going on, but to her credit, her driving to the hospital was impeccably impressive, although I never complimented her at the time, funny enough.

We arrived at the door of A&E at the City Hospital, and I literally fell out of the car. A nurse saw me and quickly grabbed a wheelchair. I was taken into the reception area and into a nearby room to wait for the medical team. The doctor was with me very quickly and they got me on a drip immediately and started carrying out all the standard tests. I had been through this drill before but wasn't enjoying it any better the second time. I was hysterical at this stage, and concerned as I was getting palpitations and my breathing was a problem. The medical team gave me some tablets to calm me down, which did help – I think.

After approximately forty-five minutes when things had settled slightly, the doctor came in to say that the tests had come back and everything was clear. He said I needed to settle down and try to relax, and that I had nothing to worry about; all should be okay. *Here we go again, have I heard this before somewhere? Where do they get these numbskull doctors?* Here was the second doctor in two weeks saying there was nothing wrong with me. He was more or less saying that my symptoms were due to stress and anxiety, and that I would be right as rain very soon. Did these guys think I was making this nonsense up?

I knew there was something seriously wrong with me and didn't need some smart-arsed doctor's diagnosis to confirm it for me, and better still, insinuate that I was imagining things.

"Get me out of this place! I bloody hate hospitals, Kate, especially on a Saturday night!" That summed up how I felt about the whole excursion. What a nightmare and completely fruitless journey. As we drove home, I was just glad that fair enough, the tests were clear, and at least the doctor was of the opinion I would be okay. Maybe I was not going to drop dead after all. I just wanted to go home, pull the duvet over my head, and never wake up.

As I lay in bed that night staring at the ceiling with the crisp moonlight shining in through the bedroom windows, I had many feelings running through my mind. Two doctors in two weeks had said I should be fine and not to worry, yet why did I feel so bloody bad? Over the next few days, my symptoms remained the same, and I was so looking forward to meeting the neurologist—at least this was the one guy in the world who might be able to tell me what the hell was happening to me.

It was Tuesday morning, and I was sort of excited, as I would be meeting the neurologist in a few hours. When I walked into the reception of his office, I met someone I knew and his wife. We acknowledged each other; however, his wife was in tears so we didn't stop to have a conversation, which suited me in any case, as I wasn't exactly full of the joys of spring myself. For some reason, there was quite an eerie feeling about the place, but I couldn't put my finger on it. As we sat in the waiting room, strangely enough, I saw another guy I knew who was there supporting his wife who was in with the neurologist. I knew this guy very well, and we chatted about football, old times, and life in general. I had heard the rumours going around that his wife suffered from multiple sclerosis, and I had pieced together that she must have been up for an appointment with the neurologist herself.

About thirty minutes later, a fit looking, sharp, smart, and casually dressed man appeared in front of me and invited me into his office. Dr. Watt was a very interesting man, quite small in stature, and came across as being very clever, educated, and extremely focused and professional. There was little small talk and he got straight to the point, and my first impressions where that I thought I liked this guy.

"So tell me what happened to you, Conor?" As I started taking Dr. Watt through the experience of the last few weeks, he listened very attentively to me and scribbled some notes while looking at me intermittently, making eye contact. I can only assume he was assessing me in every way to work out what had gone wrong. After about seven minutes of listening to me, there were a few minutes of silence as Dr. Watt finished taking his notes and flicked through some other pieces of medical information he had in front of him.

"What has likely happened, Conor, is that you have picked up some form of virus whilst travelling to Mauritius or when you just arrived, and it has caused havoc in your central nervous system. Your nervous system has come under a serious attack—an exacerbation—and this has caused a lot of nerve damage, which has resulted in your current symptoms and health problems. It's quite unfortunate, but sometimes it does happen to people, and on this occasion, that unlucky person happens to be you. When this happens for the first time, we refer to it as Myelitis."

As I sat listening to this medical expert who was now really impressing me with his knowledge and directness, I was intrigued by what he was telling me. I am a very inquisitive person by nature, and what Dr. Watt was explaining to me sounded a little mad, but at least for the first time since my attack, he was the only medical person in the world who made some sense. I felt somewhat relieved that finally a medic acknowledged that there was something wrong with me and something did happen, which was brilliant in a way, as at least I wasn't imagining things after all!

Dr. Watt had a good air of authority about him, and as a professionally qualified guy myself, I definitely respected him almost immediately and sensed that he was one of the top guys in his field. He brought a lot of sense to an otherwise crazy situation, and I got some comfort from the fact that finally I was with the right medical professional and in the right place. He went on to explain to me that it can be a very slow process for the body to recover from such an attack and that it may take up to two years for my body to make a full recovery and settle down.

If there was no recovery within this timeframe, he felt that any further recovery or improvement in my health would be unlikely. One thing that was worrying me was the fact that he said it was possible that I may experience further attacks and that if this were the case, there would be a strong possibility that I was developing a condition called multiple sclerosis. He then qualified this by saying it was far too early to talk about that. When he said the words multiple sclerosis, I sort of froze. Over the past two weeks, this was one of the conditions I kept reading about whenever I investigated my symptoms online, and it seemed a very nasty serious disease for which there was no cure. My very limited knowledge of MS and MS patients was that I believed everyone diagnosed ended up in a wheelchair at some point. The sheer thought of this outcome scared the living daylights out of me, but it was information overload at this stage so I knew I needed some time to reflect and to stay calm.

I asked him about a million and one questions, and to be fair to Dr. Watt, he was very helpful and tried his best to answer them all and make me feel at ease. After about forty minutes, I left the practice and walked to the car. Kate was with me, and in some ways, we were a little satisfied that at least we had some answers that explained what was happening to me. However, as I was driving up the dual carriageway, the reality of the situation started to hit home. Fear entered my mind and I started to get very worried about what the future held for Kate and me. What if I did have MS? Or, did I maybe have Motor Neuron disease, which is related to MS? Although I had just had lots of questions answered, I now had many more that required answering.

You see, I used to think like a lot of people: that when you get sick, you go to your GP, get a prescription, and collect the medication from the chemist around the corner, and after a few days, you'd be right as rain again. For the first time in my life, I was starting to understand that life, unfortunately, is a little more complicated, and things just don't always work out that way. It's amazing that most of us take our health for granted; we all expect to feel good all the time, not get sick, and live a long healthy life. Unfortunately, that may happen in films, but in real life, as I was now finding out firsthand, that was simply not the case. I was starting to understand that I had one hell of a fight on my hands, and at that time, I just didn't see me winning the battle. I was taking everything very badly because I definitely didn't want to be sick for the rest of my life. I had so much to achieve with Kate, our family, my sport, and my career—this was just too overwhelming to think about and so unfair to both of us.

I arrived back at my home on the Hills of East Belfast and went into the kitchen to make myself a cup of tea. It was about 12:00 p.m., and I really wanted to go back to work and get on with my life, but this seemed some way off at that particular moment.

We had moved into Castlegrange twelve months previously, and it was a modern townhouse on the outskirts of East Belfast. Both Kate and I loved our new home, and just before our wedding, we were full of excitement with what the future would hold for us. I made myself a cuppa and got the computer out again. I didn't want to forget all the information that Dr. Watt had given me, so I started googling all of my symptoms again to see if I could work out myself what the hell was wrong with me. Myelitis, he had called it. I came across a condition called Transverse Myelitis, and I really did have a lot of the symptoms of this one. However, the longer I remained on the computer, with the range of symptoms I had right now, you could have linked me with over a hundred conditions, and to be honest, my head was in a complete spin for the rest of the afternoon.

I rang my mum and we spoke for about an hour on the phone. My mum has always supported me and is the classic mother hen to all of her children. She was the best mum in the world and I did find a lot of comfort from just talking things through with her on this occasion. I could sense though that she was very concerned by what was going on with me, and it wasn't until a few years later that I found out that the onset of my illness had a very bad effect on both my mum and my dad at that time.

Over the next few weeks, Kate was back at work and I spent most of my time during the day on the computer in forums, asking questions, googling conditions, and looking for answers. It was a particularly tough time and I felt so bad, so isolated, and so sad. My whole life felt as if it was possibly over, and from a mental point of view, I was in a desperate position and sliding deeper into hopelessness and a state of depression.

As I was becoming more anxious, even the basic everyday tasks were now an issue for me as my walking was quite poor, the pressure in my head was very uncomfortable, and electrical shocks were flashing through my body continuously, scaring the living daylights out of me on each occasion. It's amazing when you are healthy how much you take for granted even the simplest of tasks. I was really struggling on a daily basis, and even going to the local supermarket was a problem. When I was on my own, which was far too often as Kate had to work, I spent most of my time just thinking of all the problems that lay ahead for me. I was really struggling to work out how I was going to cope with things if this thing, whatever the hell it was, didn't clear off.

The one thing I couldn't get my head around was that generally over the past thirty-odd years I had managed to stay clear of any sort of illness. I had an episode of glandular fever when I was five years old where I pretty much missed the whole of my first year at school. However, apart from that, I was healthy, extremely sporty, and very active, which added to the shock of what was happening to my body now as a young man.

It became clearer that my days of playing sport and keeping fit and healthy through sport were over, and this was particularly difficult to accept in those early days. My mother informs me I first started kicking a ball at the age of two, and from a young age, I was into most sports and excelled particularly in both Gaelic football and soccer. I won an all-Ireland medal representing the University of Ulster at Gaelic football, and won several honours playing soccer, to include participation in three Milk Cup tournaments, captaining N. Ireland at underage level, and trials with Coventry City in England. The highlight of them all was playing for Ireland in the World Student Games in Beijing China in 2002. I also played Irish league football for the previous ten years, so as you can see, sport was a massive part of my development and my life In general. It was now very difficult trying to accept the fact that as a result of this illness, or whatever it was, I may never be able to play or enjoy sport again.

I was suffering every day at this point with panic attacks and heart palpitations. If you have never experienced either if these problems, believe me, you don't want to. To put it in layman's terms, when I was getting a panic attack and palpitations, I felt as if I was about to die. When you are getting these every day over a sustained period of time, it is terrifying, and the amount of stress both physical, and even more so, mental that my body was under was almost unbearable. I now believe looking back at this part of my life that I went through a mini breakdown throughout the first twelve months of initial symptoms.

My GP was great and very supportive. He ordered me to stay in close contact with him so that he could monitor my situation. For the panic attacks, he prescribed some medication to help me stay calm; however, I only stayed on it for a few days as the tablets slowed me down to almost robotic pace, and they were messing with my head so I threw them in the bin. I am not really into medication and tablets in general, and if there was an alternative therapy that would help me, I would prefer to take that route. Someone close to me suggested acupuncture as it came highly recommended; however, I still cannot work out to this day how needles being inserted into various parts of the body are supposed to be relaxing. Someone must be having a laugh with that one. Needless to say, I didn't stick with the acupuncture for too long; however, if you are reading this and find that it works for you, good luck to you, but I will be passing on that form of therapy for the time being.

As I mentioned previously, I have always been quite spiritual and have great faith, so I started to explore the possibility of finding a good faith healer who may be able to heal me. There have been lots of miracles both witnessed and recorded over the years, and I did believe, and more so hoped, that maybe I would be next.

Ireland is famous for its faith healers, as over the years there has been many stories where people are supposed to have been cured by such people. At this point in my life, I was prepared to try anything if I thought it would help, so I started to make some enquiries into whom I should go and see. We came across a faith healer who had a great reputation in Co. Mayo and we made an appointment for the following weekend. This man apparently had a great success rate, and I was excited about meeting him, as I believed there was a real chance he could get my body back to normal again.

The following weekend, we drove the long five-hour journey to the west of Ireland to Castlebar full of hope. My symptoms were as bad as ever and my form was desperately low. We booked into a hotel in the center of the town on a Friday night, as the appointment was early Saturday morning. I had a very restless night's sleep as the pressure in my head was annoying me and the electric shocks were relentless.

The next morning, we got up early and went down to the restaurant to have some breakfast. I wasn't overly hungry and was just excited at the fact that there was a chance that I was going to see a man very shortly who might be able to fix me. When we arrived at the house, I went in alone and there were about ten people from all over Ireland in the living room, which had now become a waiting room. People from all walks of life were there, waiting to see this great healer who would hopefully cure them of all sorts of health problems, including cancer and other very serious life threatening cases. There were two people present in wheelchairs, and I was wondering if they had MS, but I wasn't going to be so rude as to ask them. Anyway, it didn't matter, as all I wanted was for the man to get me sorted so I could get my life back and get back to work.

After waiting what seemed closer to three days but was more accurately about an hour, I was called as the next patient, so I went in and met this great healer for the first time. The man himself was an eccentric type of character, very chatty and extremely confident in what he was doing. He carried out his healing process in the kitchen and spent approximately thirty minutes treating me. He was a pleasant enough man and he started working on my body, massaging oil deep into the skin and talking me through my symptoms. He told me that I had some form of virus and that with his help and God's help I would be back on my feet again in three to four weeks.

He was very convincing, and off course, I was hoping that his prediction was true. For a short period of time, he did lift my form and gave me some hope— something that I really needed at that stage in my life. I made a donation of fifty euros, and he said he wanted to see me again in two weeks' time. As I left, I was feeling a lot more enthusiastic about my chances of recovery and was glad that I had made the effort to drive the long journey to get cured. On leaving the house, I got an opportunity to speak with some of the other people, and the word on this guy was great; so overall, I was very optimistic that my journey was worthwhile. As I got back in the car, I explained the experience to Kate as we made our way back to the hotel to get some lunch. She was delighted, but probably more so from hearing me being a little positive for a change.

That night we decided to go for a quiet meal and a few drinks in Castlebar town centre. I was feeling really bad about the whole illness at this stage, although Kate never complained; I knew full well she was very worried and annoyed about everything. She has never actually sat me down and explained to me what she was thinking at that time, but it must have been so hard for her to cope and stick with me in those early days.

We got back to the hotel and had some lunch. I sipped on a pint of Guinness, my favorite tipple, purely for medicinal reasons. We agreed to go out for a few drinks later that evening if I felt a bit better. I wasn't really feeling any better, but I agreed to go out anyway as it wasn't fair on Kate not to. We had heard there were a few good pubs in the town, so we agreed to go to a local pub across the road, as it was a short walk, which suited me very well. It was a Saturday night and the bar was full of couples and revelers all letting their hair down, enjoying the excellent sounds of a very good traditional Irish band. Everyone seemed in great form, apart from me that is, but I was really trying to put a brave face on, even though I was still feeling like shit. The pressure in my head was building up and I started feeling extremely unwell again. I said so to Kate and she suggested we go back to the hotel. Then all of a sudden, I got a huge pain in my chest that nearly knocked me off the seat. I told Kate that I needed a doctor quick and she asked at the bar, and luckily, for us, there was a doctor's surgery open during the weekend in the town based just across the road. We very quickly made a beeline for the surgery.

We ran in and I demanded to see the doctor immediately, as my heart was pumping and head close to exploding. Almost immediately, the doctor came out to see me and we had a conversation. He thought he should give me a Valium shot as I was in a bad state of panic, so I agreed, and he injected some into my left arm. A few minutes after the shot, I started to settle, thankfully. The medication obviously worked and things seemed a little better. The doctor carried out all the usual tests, and guess what? After about thirty minutes, he said I was fine, that there was nothing irregular, and I just needed to try to relax and stay calm. He advised me to get some rest, so we set sail for the hotel and I went straight to bed. I had ruined another night for Kate and was in bed before 10:00 p.m. What was going on with me? When the hell was this ever going to end? So much for the bloody faith healer — what a waste of fifty euros.

The next morning, we went down for breakfast. I was really disappointed with the trip to Castlebar after what had happened the night before. To be fair to the faith healer, he did say that I might get worse before I started to feel better, and he told me that after about three weeks, I should be in good shape again. I thought that maybe I was being too hard on myself, and maybe I would be healed but it would take a few weeks as he said. As we got back in the car and started the five-hour drive back to Belfast, I was hoping that I was going to improve and tried my best to be as positive as possible.

Two weeks later, I felt no better; my symptoms were still bad and I was generally feeling like crap. The past fortnight had been a disaster, and my symptoms, if anything, had got worse instead of better. I had cursed the faith healer up and down and had accepted the fact that I hadn't been cured, so I made another appointment with Dr. Watt, as I had so many more questions for him.

I went back to Dr. Watt and it was more of the same, really. He had a number of questions for me and he was scribbling on his note pad as he went through his file. I asked again, what was happening to me, and he basically repeated what he had said the first time. He told me that I would need to take some time off work, maybe three to six months as it was a slow process, and the only thing that would help me was rest. He told me to forget about playing football and going to the gym or proper exercise. He wanted me to rest up and take it easy. This was a real disappointing session — six months off work. How could I tell my employer that I might be off for six months? This surely was the end of my career. What would Kate think? What was I going to do? How would I be able to support Kate and pay the bills? I had so many more questions now, but we had run out of time so I returned home.

I walked upstairs and just fell flat on the bed. It was about 12:00 p.m. and I was lying looking at the ceiling. Kate was at work, as usual, so I was all alone just thinking of what I was going to do. For the first time since my honeymoon, I started to believe that I was very ill and there may be no comeback. I was probably going to have to resign from my job and my career would be over. I was only married a number of months, but I was lying here today and all of my dreams were in the bin. As I tried to visualize what it would be like to grow old and very sick from this day forward, I could feel a small tear starting to roll down my cheek for the first time. Like many men, I am very private with my feelings and crying is not something I do on a regular basis; in fact, I don't cry—period. As the tears were rolling down my cheeks, I was officially devastated. All alone in this lovely house, very ill at the grand old age of twenty-eight years old—all I could think was *Why me? What have I done, God, to deserve this?* It was so unfair.

Attitude is a little thing that makes a big difference.
—*Winston Churchill*

CHAPTER 3   MRI RESULTS

Over the course of the next nine months, my symptoms remained more or less the same. I had been to see Dr. Watt a few times, and had experienced no improvement at all as far as I was concerned. In fact, at times I felt as if my condition was getting worse. One thing that was really concerning me was that I had developed a very weird problem in my throat that was causing me a lot of distress and annoyance. It went on for a number of months, and I had been up to the Ulster hospital a couple of times to get it checked out, but the tests came back clear. I was very fortunate that my great friend James had introduced me to Dr. Mc Govern who was one of the top doctors in the hospital. Over the previous months when I was quite ill, I had to make some emergency visits to the hospital. Dr. Mc Govern was brilliant with me, and each time made me feel at ease and calmed my nerves a little at a very difficult time.

Another important development at this time was that I had decided to go back to work in an attempt to get a little normality back into my life. My boss, Mr. Wheeler, was fantastic with me, and the arrangement I had with him was that if I wasn't feeling great, I was allowed to go home and rest. This was a huge breakthrough for me, as I don't think I could have handled the situation if my employer hadn't been as supportive. The thing is, when you are faced with a terrible illness and life is very difficult, it is important to have a sympathetic employer. I was very fortunate that this was the case, as I know of others who are not so fortunate. From a financial point of view, it was also very helpful, as my salary was still being paid in full, and therefore I was able to support Kate and pay the bills. This was obviously very important at that time and certainly relieved some of the stress I was feeling.

A year had passed since my first attack on honeymoon and I had another appointment booked in with Dr. Watt on 21st August 2007 at the Ulster Clinic in Belfast. This was an important date as it was also my twenty-ninth birthday. I hadn't seen him in a few months, and I felt in my bones that this was an important appointment. I had undertaken a second MRI scan a week before my appointment, and I was very worried and a little apprehensive and nervous as to what he was going to tell me had shown up on the scan.

I didn't sleep great the night before the appointment, and as I got out of bed that morning, I was feeling very tense. It was a beautiful day outside for a change, but all I could think of was my appointment with Dr. Watt at the clinic. My appointment was at 10:00 a.m. and as I wanted to get up in good time, I made my way up early. The Ulster Clinic is a very busy place with lots of doctors, nurses, visitors, and patients all frantically moving about. As I waited outside Dr. Watts's door, I was hoping that maybe I was in for some good news for a change. A few minutes later, the door opened and I went in, and Dr. Watt asked me to take a seat.

"Good Morning, Conor, how have you been feeling these past few months?" he asked. I went on to tell him that my symptoms were up and down and that I was worried about lots of things, including my throat. He was familiar with the throat problem and advised me that it was likely a result of all the stress and anxiety in my body; he also said that potentially I had an acid reflux problem.

"Conor, your MRI scans have come back, and I have to tell you that it is not good news, unfortunately. The truth is you have a number of new lesions in your brain, as you can see on the scans I have in my hand. Having monitored your symptoms over the past twelve months, and looking at the most recent MRI scan, I can now confirm, Conor, that you are suffering from multiple sclerosis, and you will have it for the rest of your life. There are a number of disease modifying drugs available, and I would recommend that you start a course right away. What do you think?"

I hadn't time to think, but over the last sixty seconds, I could physically feel the blood draining from my face. Did he just diagnose me with multiple sclerosis? Did I hear him correctly?

"Yes, whatever you think Dr. Watt. I will start a course—what do you recommend?"

"I think you should go with Rebiff —a Beta interferon. It's one of the more popular ones, and I think you should give it a go."

"No problem; I will start it right away."

I asked Dr. Watt a few questions, and he then said he wanted to see me in three months' time, and in the meantime, he advised me to just take it easy and try to relax. I left his office and started the walk back to my car in a bit of a daze, I might add. I got into the car and just sat there for about twenty minutes, when a couple of tears started to run down my cheek. *I have MS and will have it for the rest of my life. My life is definitely over now—my job, my football, my family—I'll never have children and my dreams have completely evaporated over the past fifteen minutes.*

I just sat there distraught and feeling as if hell had opened and swallowed me up. I was immersed in negative thoughts and felt as though I was being suffocated by so many dark feelings. I was still in shock, but I had better hurry up and get used to it, as this MS thing was not going to go away. I had just been diagnosed with one of the worst neurological conditions to affect young adults, and there was nothing I or anyone else could do about it.

After my initial reaction of shock and a few tears, I took a deep breath and reflected a little. I felt so alone, so lost, and so sad. Kate was at home waiting for me, and I knew I should call her immediately, but I couldn't face that call so I decided to just wait for another few moments. I mean, I did know there was something badly wrong with me, but ever the optimist, I was sort of hoping that Dr. Watt would give me the all clear and I could move on with my life and eventually return to normal. Unfortunately, that was not going to happen now. I would consider myself a good person, had lived my short life as best I could, and felt as though I certainly did not deserve this. It started to hit me that from that day onward, my life was going to change.

I lifted my mobile phone and made the call I dreaded; I phoned my mum to give her the bad news. When my mum answered the phone, I told her that the appointment was not good news and that Dr. Watt had diagnosed me with multiple sclerosis. I think she was shocked and completely devastated, but she tried to encourage me to be positive and promised me that she would pray very hard to Our Lady and that one day, I would be cured. I listened to her for a few moments, but I didn't have the strength to talk to her much longer, not now; I needed some time to gather my thoughts.

I told her that I needed to go and would speak with her later. I hung up and took a deep breath. Making that phone call was one of the hardest things I have ever had to do. I knew my mum and dad had been heartbroken ever since I rang them from Mauritius twelve months previous to tell them I had been admitted to the hospital. It was particularly hard on them, and I suppose you can only realize this pain when you have children yourself. The next call I made was to my sister Ciara. Ciara is six years older than I am, and since I was a little boy, she has been looking over me to this very day. We have always been close over the years, and she is one of the people in my life who have truly inspired me. When I told her about my diagnosis, I knew she was absolutely devastated. It was a really hard call, but I didn't want to talk for too long so I cut it short again, hung up, and headed for home listening to some Damian Rice just to top off the somber mood.

I arrived back at home a short time later, and as I pulled into the driveway, I could see Kate's car. She was waiting for me so I needed to sharpen myself up and try to be positive. I didn't want Kate to see me distraught, so I tried to pull myself together. I walked in and Kate was in the living room.

I came right to the point. "Well I got some bad news; I've got multiple sclerosis."

Kate's facial expression said it all—she was flabbergasted and as completely devastated as I was. There was silence for about thirty-seconds while we just looked at each other distraught, both in pieces, and both still in a state of shock. We then hugged each other for what seemed like an hour and cried with no chat whatsoever. Since the onset of my illness on our honeymoon, Kate had been fantastic with me and supported me every single hour of every single day. It was her strength that really drove me on. I promised myself and her right there and then that one day I would beat this shit, and pay her back for all the support she gave me. It was a release of one year's anger, tension, and questions, but I was just so happy that I was with the women I loved, and for a few minutes, we just said nothing and continued with our hug.

I was glad in a way, I suppose, that I was finally diagnosed with something. It had been one very difficult year, and over the past twelve months, it felt at times as if some people thought I was making this entire thing up. So many hospital visits, so many unexplained symptoms, and so many doctors had told me I was fine, and all along I knew I wasn't. So much for the medic's then—negligence of the highest order in my view.

I have MS and there is nothing I can do about it, and it's as simple as that, so I had better get used to it.

The remainder of that day was very quiet in the house. Kate went back to work and I had time to reflect on the events of the past year. In hindsight, it was bloody obvious I had MS. I had all the hallmarks, and I suppose I was more settled now that at least I was diagnosed and I could get the proper treatment to help me manage things. The difficulty was that every time I tried to be positive, my mind played games with me. I'd think to myself, *there is no cure for MS, and the likelihood is that I will deteriorate over the next five to ten years and be in a wheelchair by the time I am forty-five.* I could not deal with these thoughts, and my head was in a constant spin. I went to bed and lay down to rest. As I was dozing off to sleep completely wrecked with all the stress of the last twenty-four hours, I wasn't bothered if I ever woke up again. What would be the point anyway, as my life was more or less over.

Wake up I did the next morning. I had slept for over fourteen hours, which was a first for me, but I still felt like crap. That day I went to see my GP and gave him the bad news. I was also feeling worse than usual, so he prescribed me another course of steroids. The problem with people who have MS is that there are higher levels of inflammation swimming around the body attacking the central nervous system at it's leisure. One way to bring this to a halt is to manage the inflammation. Steroids are the most common medication designed to deal with this. This must have been my fourth course in the past twelve months, and I wasn't keen on taking them again as there are side effects, like there are with most medications, that I particularly didn't enjoy. I took them anyway as I was feeling pretty bad, and sure, what the hell was there to lose?

I found the first few months of my MS diagnosis extremely difficult. I was feeling rough most days and my balance and walking was particularly bad. I was a twenty-nine-year-old young man living in what felt like a seventy-nine-year-old man's body. MS sufferers will understand this, but I felt terrible most of the time. I mean, I looked sort of fine on the outside, but the reality was, I felt really sick most days, which was upsetting me a lot. It was crushing my dreams and hopes for any sort of future. I was still going to work most days, but was finding it very difficult and tiring having to put a brave face on things when concerned colleagues asked me how I was feeling and questions around what had actually happened to me. I had put on some weight as a result of the medication, and this along with zero exercise was taking its toll on me. Apart from work, I very rarely left the house.

My symptoms at that time were severe nerve pain, crazy balance problems, panic attacks, throat problems, and I had this chronic stress-like pressure in my head, which was really concerning me. My mental health was not good and I certainly wasn't great company as each day I felt as if I was slipping deeper and deeper into a darker hole. I was still in a state of disbelief and did not really accept my diagnosis—certainly not in those very early days. I could not believe that twelve months after I got married, this could possibly happen to someone like me. I mean, I knew exactly what was going on, but sometimes it was so surreal that it felt as if everything was just a bad dream—if only that were the case.

It was coming up to Christmas, and my first as an officially diagnosed fully-fledged MSer. The previous year I had spent most of Christmas day in bed, coming downstairs in my mum's house only for my dinner. This year we were spending Christmas day in my in-laws house, and again I wasn't looking forward to it at all, as I was feeling really rough, and celebrating was the last thing on my mind. As far as I was concerned, I didn't have anything to celebrate anyway. We always spend a few days at Christmas visiting our friends and relatives in Cookstown, but this year I just wasn't in the form. Christmas came and went, and to be fair I put a brave face on things for the sake of everyone else. I didn't want to ruin everyone's celebrations, so I was telling Kate and my close family circle that I was feeling ok. I think they were aware of how I was really feeling; however, they never mentioned anything, which made it a little easier for me.

Over the course of the next few months, I had to change my medication on the instruction of Dr. Watt. There are a number of disease modifying drugs you can take for MS and off the back of his recommendations, initially I chose Rebiff. However, very quickly we worked out that I had to get off it, as it wasn't agreeing with my body at all and actually made me very sick. Copaxone was offered to me as the next best thing so I agreed to get on it immediately. Basically, Copaxone is taken daily in the form of an injection. I hated needles like most people, but if this stuff could make me better or prevent attacks in the future, I was prepared to give it a go. Thankfully, the Copaxone seemed to agree with my body quite quickly, so I was a little happier that with a bit of luck, I was now on the right medication at the very least. My form, however, at this time was still very bad, and as I injected each day over the next few months, I felt very sorry for myself. I still couldn't believe I had this bastard of a disease, and better still; the fact that I would be injecting for the rest of my life was putting my head away. When injecting daily, it is important that you vary the injection sites due to bruising. I now have a few favorite sites, mostly on my backside and waist, as there is more body fat there, hence less of a nip.

The other major problem that I couldn't get my head around at this stage of my illness was the fact that I wasn't going to be able to play football again. This might seem trivial to many, but to me at this stage, it was breaking my heart. Both my GP and my neurologist told me that my football days were over, and this was very hard to take at that time. The only exercise I was advised to do was short walks, and even then, I needed to be very careful. I found this extremely difficult to accept, and there was a small flame in my heart still flickering that said to me this was a load of baloney, and if it were the last thing I did—I would be back playing football and back at the gym, at some point in the future.

On that delightful thought, my first task was to get my head right. Mental health problems are rife in the world today. It's something that I have never really thought about before. Until I got sick, I had taken my health for granted like most people in the world. However, it's not until to you are sick that you realize the amount of people who are in a similar position. Mental health problems, for me, are the silent killer. You could look great on the outside, and when in conversation with others put up a great act, but in private, you are in absolute bits. You have lost all form of hope and are merely getting through the days. Around this time, approximately eighteen months into my illness, was about the first time I started to get suicidal thoughts.

I am very happy to discuss this as it's a very serious issue and very real, but for whatever reason, I started to look into this whole area, maybe even to see if I could understand why people go down this route. I wasn't what I would describe as suicidal; however, the thought started to flick through my mind now and again and I was just really confused. MS, broadly speaking, cannot kill you, and the frightening thing is that I was advised by a specialist that suicide is one of the main killers in people with MS, of which I was very aware of through my research. I have always been a deep thinker, so I would be being untruthful to you if I didn't share the fact that these thoughts were at times flickering through my mind. Every day I was trying my best to be positive, and at times, I was, but the negative aspect of the situation I found myself in would supersede the positives at this stage in my illness. This is the period of my illness that I was certainly at rock bottom.

The days and nights passed by and my symptoms more or less stayed the same. I was sick to death with everything and could feel myself slipping into a depressive state of hopelessness. I felt at times that I had joined the living dead, as I could see no light at the end of the tunnel. The deeper I fell into my depressive state, the worse my MS symptoms seemed to get. Very simple daily chores like going to the supermarket and meeting people either at work or otherwise was a struggle. Everyone meant well, but I was sick to death of people inquiring about my health now and having to talk about it, and explain what happened to me.

At this point, the general public still didn't really know what was up with me other than I hadn't been well. My close friends and family knew I got very sick on honeymoon and was still quite bad, but most were not aware of my diagnosis.

Irish families are well renowned for keeping sickness and illness private and within family. It seems to be a cardinal sin to discuss your illness or diagnosis outside the immediate family, and our family was no different. My mum felt it was important and no one's business, and that we kept my diagnosis confidential. Some rumours had got back to me, and I remember my brother Colm saying he was told by another guy from my hometown that the word on the street and the Gaelic club was I had multiple sclerosis. Colm, the good loyal sport he is, just denied it and said I was back to full health. I suppose they were trying to protect me, and it was a very personal thing that I didn't want anyone finding out anyway at that particular time.

I have two younger brothers, Colm two years my junior and Barry four years younger who is the baby of the family. Both lads are great fellas and we had a fantastic time growing up in Lomond heights in Cookstown along with Ciara and our Corgi Brandy and mum and dad. Both Colm and Barry were also very good at sports, and when we were young boys, the three of us spent every hour God sent kicking a ball around the place. I know when I got sick, initially the lads were very upset, but it was something we never really talked about and still really don't. Barry emigrated to Australia a few years earlier and was making a new life for himself there, and Colm was getting married soon so it was all go for both boys on a personal front in the middle of my illness.

I suppose as the eldest boy in the house, I tried to look after the boys when we were all growing up and I can honestly say that although we fought away growing up and argued a lot over silly stuff like normal brothers, there is a strong bond between us and we look out for one another, to this day. The difference now was that I was in trouble with this illness, and I think both boys, like everyone else, were feeling rather helpless. That's the thing about illness; there is very little anyone can do but be supportive and try to help out where they can.

Approximately two years after my first attack, I was still very much in a bad place. My tyres were firmly flat and I was worried for all sorts of reasons. I still hadn't accepted my illness and I was very concerned of what the future held for

Kate and me. How was my career going to pan out? Would I ever have children? Would Kate leave me? Would I be in a wheelchair soon? So many questions with little to no answers. Hope was something I always had. I was always a bubbly, confident guy; however, my MS diagnoses had knocked me for six and left me with an empty feeling. Hope had been replaced with hopelessness.

A challenge only becomes an obstacle when you bow to it....
— AUTHOR UNKNOWN

CHAPTER 4   DREAMERS MOVE MOUNTAINS

It was a wet Saturday morning, and as I looked out through the window with the rain beating hard against it, I was trying to work out whether I would go to a business conference in a hotel close by. Over the past few months, I had been trying my very best to keep my mind occupied and one of the ways that helped me achieve this was to look at a number of different business opportunities. I was worried about my career in property, and as I have always been quite ambitious and entrepreneurial, I was always on the lookout for new business ideas and concepts. The economy was in a recession in Ireland, one of the worst to hit in over fifty years, and I was getting more and more concerned about my ability to make money and support my family should my health deteriorate.

Two weeks previous, a friend of mine had invited me to a conference where the guest speaker was a Scottish entrepreneur. He was apparently excellent and this would be the only time he would be in Northern Ireland. I was unsure as to whether I was going to attend or not, as my form was particularly bad the previous week, and combined with the miserable weather, I couldn't really be bothered leaving the house if I was being honest. However, around mid-day I pulled myself together, and as the conference started at 1:00 p.m. I decided to take a run up to see what was going on.

The keynote speaker was a Mr. Bert Jukes, who was described as a motivational business guru, and one of the finest entrepreneurs to come out of Scotland in recent years. Quite a build-up, and I was looking forward to hearing what this guy had to say.

The conference commenced at 1:30 p.m. and Mr. Jukes came onto the stage and introduced himself with one of the largest smiles I've ever seen. I liked the look of this guy almost immediately and what stood out was his sense of humour combined with genuine charisma. Charisma is something you cannot teach or give to someone, and is a quality in a person that I believe you are born with. It was very obvious that this Bert guy had bundles of it and he really worked the room well, as he went through his presentation over the next sixty minutes.

The talk was called Dreamers Move Mountains, and Bert was very focused on sharing his experiences over the past twenty-five years with all in attendance. His core message was that if you believed more in yourself and put in place a plan for your life, you can achieve what you want to achieve in life. He shared with us that in life, everyone has their own mountain to climb but that if you dig in and get a plan in place, dreamers can move mountains. His view was that if people dreamt and believed in themselves more, then their own dreams might just come true.

He talked about subject matter that I had never really heard of before, a thing called personal development. He advised us that if we embraced personal development, then what we wanted out of life, the universe would make sure it happens. He shared with us his views on people and conversation and suggested that when people ask how you are doing, you tell them you are terrific. Even if you are not, tell them anyway. He said the most common Northern Ireland response to the question "How are you?" was, "I'm not too bad?"

"What the hell does that mean?" he asked. "Tell them you are terrific." To be fair, he made a lot of sense and everyone in the room was transfixed with Bert's presentation and his very unique form of delivery. In short, the whole experience moved me that day and switched a light on in my mind. For the first time since my initial symptoms, I started to consider that maybe if I approached my own situation in a more positive manner, things might just improve a little. I started to ask some questions of myself, and sat there thinking, *You know what? I might conquer my own mountains if I put a plan in place and just believed I would get better*.

After the talk, I went up to Bert and introduced myself through the crowd. It would have been easier getting an autograph of one of the guys from Westlife with the amount of people trying to speak to Bert, but I persevered, managed to give him my card, and told him that if he ever needed any property help in Northern Ireland, to give me a call. We talked for a few minutes, and then I headed for home. I was just pleased that he seemed interested in me and gave me some of his time.

One of the most interesting things about that morning was that I hadn't really noticed my symptoms, so I was wondering to myself, *how the hell does that work*. As I drove home, I had a spring in my step, and for the first time in ages, I was feeling very positive and it felt great. I felt that after three years of hell, it was about time that I started taking control of my life and stopped feeling sorry for myself. I was feeling very positive and was looking forward to getting home to go on-line and buy some of the books Bert had recommended I started to read.

Personal development includes activities that improve awareness and identity, develop talents and potential, build human capital, and facilitate employability. It enhances quality of life and contributes to the realiza- tion of dreams and aspirations. The concept is not limited to self-help, but includes formal and informal activities for developing others in roles such as teacher, guide, counselor, manager, coach, or mentor.

I was fairly well educated and had an excellent job, but where had I been all these years that no one had mentioned these two words to me before. From that day forward my personal development journey began, and to this day is a massive part in my daily life and will be until I leave this planet. Since that day over three years ago, I have been very fortunate to develop a close friendship with Bertie; he has helped me develop on a personal and entrepreneurial level over the past few years, and has encouraged me to keep pushing myself and strive to be the best I can be.

This is a good example of taking control of a situation and taking action which I talk a lot more about later in the book. As a result of me deciding to get off my backside that Saturday morning and going to the talk, so many good things have happened in my life, and I have continued my personal development journey, which is fantastic and has paid dividends. As you are reading this, there may also be things and opportunities for you to meet people and get involved in projects. My advice is to get out there and do it. Go talk to that guy you are not sure about, make that telephone call you don't want to, and go to that meeting you couldn't really be bothered going to. It could change your life as it has done to mine on more than one occasion.

I was still taking my Copaxone, and the following week, for the first time in nearly two years, I decided to join the gym in Belfast. This was a huge step for me as I felt it was important I try to get a level of fitness back as I had literally done nothing since the onset of my symptoms. Over the past number of months through researching MS on the Internet, I had come across a number of people who had very encouraging and inspirational stories in relation to their own battles with MS. One guy I came across in particular was a Mr. Montel Williams.

I knew this guy from the television when I was quite young, as I used to watch his morning TV chat show in years gone by. He was an American talk show host and very famous in his own right. Montel had suffered from MS for the past twenty years. He was a MS champion fighter and had written a number of books and publications about his daily fight against the illness. Over the course of the next few months, I started to study the guy, and read his material to get an idea of how he was fighting and beating MS. I found his whole story inspirational and it restored my hope in life and re-enforced my new thinking that I could possibly beat this thing and turn my life around. It was amazing how Montel had described how bad he was feeling live on television and how no one else had known what he was going through. His feet were in so much pain at times that he used to go to his dressing room after the show and physically cry. I could relate to a lot of this stuff because for the past few years, I had felt like crap, but the only person who really knew this was me, as I looked pretty normal on the outside. In the early years, he kept his condition a secret and suffered in silence. He also suffered from suicidal thoughts and was moments from ending it all by throwing himself in front of a vehicle.

I could relate to the guy. His literature introduced me to a new school of thought and inspired me to get back to the gym and get fit. I worked out that MS was generally accepted as a progressive disease, and over time, the prognosis was that your body would deteriorate. He advised all MS'ers that if they could, they should build up their strength and try and get as fit as possible so that the body is stronger for the fight in the years to come. This all made perfect sense, and I knew this is exactly what I needed to do if I wanted to try to beat this thing.

I could feel in my bones and in my mind that I was now entering a new phase in my illness and my life. Studying the condition and realizing that other people were fighting similar battles and winning gave me back some hope. I started to believe in myself more, and through my spirit and great faith in god, I believed for the first time that I would get better. I firmly started to work on my plan, and the plan was to simply get my life back and beat this invader. I was sick to death with everything MS, so I was going to commit to whatever I had to do that would help me beat it.

I started to work on my strength and fitness and attended the gym regularly. It was fantastic to be back at the gym, and over the next few months, I tried to make two visits per week. At the beginning, it was really difficult and there were days when my symptoms were so bad that I would have to cut my session early and just go home quite deflated. Those days were the toughest, and the little green man on my shoulder would be whispering very quietly in my ear, "Conor, you have MS, you shouldn't be at the gym and you will deteriorate very soon, so just give up."

However, on the other shoulder, there was another little man who was telling me to keep going and forget about Mr. Negative Head across the way. This analogy is a constant occurrence I have found in my life and I believe is present in every-one's lives. Most people have a negative and positive outlook on lots of things, and I believe you should only feed the positive side of the brain and flush out the negative. The problem with the world today is that there is so much negativity around; it is very difficult to remain in a positive frame of mind. If you pick up a daily newspaper any day of the week and flick through the pages, you will strug-gle to find positive news stories. It's all negative nonsense designed to corrupt your mind. Society in general needs some positive direction and encouragement to help people embrace personal development and strive to better themselves. It is now widely accepted that those who have a positive attitude towards whatever they are doing or facing in life are a lot more successful than those who have a negative outlook.

A couple of weeks later, I was sitting at home on my own as Kate was at work and the doorbell rang. I went to the door and found the postman with a delivery I had to sign for. As I opened the package, I could see very clearly that it was a book. There was a small envelope with the book and I opened it first and inside was a short note from a friend of mine that said, "Conor, have a read of this book and never give up the battle—you can win the fight, my friend" ☺. The book was called *It's Not About the Bike*, written by Lance Armstrong. I was slightly overwhelmed with this gesture from my buddy, and all I really knew of Lance Armstrong was that he was one of the best cyclists ever, and he had beaten can-cer to come back and win the Tour de France a number of times.

As I had plenty of time on my hands, I decided that I would read the book and see if I could get anything from it. Read it I did, and I have to say, if you are fighting illness and are a little lost in your life, you should read this. As I was in my first few months of severe symptoms, Lance's story really gave me some hope that I should fight whatever illness I had and that I too could win the battle. There is a divided opinion worldwide of Lance Armstrong due to the challenges and episodes he has faced in his cycling career, however one thing that is indisputable is that this guy is one hell of a fighter and his attitude is the reason in my view he is still standing on this earth today. Lances book was the perfect tonic for this stage of my challenge. It drove me on to believe that I could and should start to fight this illness.

I continued to go to the gym more regularly, and guess what? I had also started to play football again. This was another major breakthrough for me as I've touched upon, football had been a huge part of my life, and when I originally got sick, the medical team told me my football days were finished. I was asked to play for a local team, and even getting out on the grass again with proper football boots on, running around, shouting at players, scoring goals, and sharing the banter with the lads in the dressing room was absolutely terrific. Although, I still had to be careful, this was a major development in my MS story and a defining moment in terms of my confidence levels.

With my new fitness regime in place, the next thing I needed to address was my diet. I never really had an overly bad diet, as I was very into sport and tried to keep myself relatively trim over the years; however, I had learned through my MS research that diet was a very important element to people with this condition. The food and drink you put into your body gives you the energy to work and play every day. The research opened my eyes to many things, and I started to watch what I ate and put more healthy options into my shopping trolley. I talk in more detail with reference to my diet later on in the book, but for the first time since diagnosis, I felt as if I was turning a corner.

Physically, my symptoms were still very difficult, but definitely from a mental point of view, I was starting to believe in myself more and the determination within me was gathering serious momentum. I had finally begun to accept my condition and had started to talk more openly about what was going on with me to others. I also started to find out that it helped me and my confidence levels, by sharing my story with a few close friends.

As I started to talk more openly about my problems, I was beginning to feel a little better about it all. My daily symptoms at this stage were still difficult, and the worst of these was undoubtedly the balance problems. I was also suffering from these random electric shocks, which in medical terms are referred to as L'hermitte's signs. It was a daily occurrence at this stage and every time it happened, it frightened me to death and was largely the reason behind my panic attacks and palpitations during that period. Thankfully, the frequency of these attacks reduced over the next few months, but they were still happening too often for my liking.

Over the course of the past year, I had made a number of visits to my neurologist. It was very difficult to track progress, but I knew that certainly in the past few months, I felt as if my body was starting to cope better with the stress of the condition. Dr. Watt seemed a little more optimistic with me at this point, as over the past two years he had seen me very ill—none more so than twelve months previous, when I was sitting in his office and took a little turn for the worse. This definitely unnerved Dr. Watt, and after taking some time and a sip of water, he had to physically walk me to my car. That was probably one of the lowest days I've ever had with my MS, but it just makes me even more grateful for my good health today.

Fast-forward twelve months to one of my quarterly appointments with Dr. Watt, where he was a lot more positive and hopeful that my condition might stabilize. With my new revised enthusiasm, diet, and exercise plan, he was hopeful that my health in general would return to a much better state. I hoped to God he was right, as I thought I deserved a break from all this crap. It would be great if I could feel normal again, even for a few days—even half a day. Overall, I was a lot more content with myself and was convinced that if I stuck to the plan of my medication, diet, and exercise, and a positive approach to the MS, I would continue to improve. This is what I fully intended to do.

Every day may not be good, but there's something good in every day.

— AUTHOR UNKNOWN

CHAPTER 5   ATTITUDE IS EVERYTHING

Over the course of the following months, my symptoms were gradually becoming a little more manageable. I was able to do more in the gym, I was on a healthy diet program, and I was reading a new book once a month, which was great. My reading, up to being introduced to personal development by Bertie, was limited to the sports pages in the daily newspaper; however, for the first time in my life, I was studying my condition, studying people who had fought and beat illness, and I had embraced personal development. From an entrepreneurial point of view, I had also decided that I was going to get my business career back on track, so I thought it prudent to start studying some of the most successful entrepreneurs the world has ever produced.

As I explained earlier, I am a chartered surveyor and worked in the property industry, and throughout the past couple of years, my employer had been extremely supportive. However, I had felt that I had reached a crossroads in my life as a professional and knew that the time was getting closer whereby I needed to make a few tough calls on my future. I have always been very entrepreneurial from a young boy, and I remember my first job very clearly, which involved collecting glasses in a local hotel for six pounds a night at the age of thirteen years old.

I remember well the first night I was paid. I had worked the Friday, Saturday, and Sunday night, and at the end of the night, I got my pay in a small envelope that held a grand total of eighteen pounds in cash, and the same again in tips. I remember feeling very proud of myself that I had a job so young, and was making my own money. It gave me a great sense of independence, which has stuck with me to this very day.

In my current day job, although I enjoyed and respected the company very much, I had felt that I had stopped growing and learning. I had progressed quite quickly in my career to date, and at the grand old age of twenty-eight years old I was already a director in a very successful Northern Ireland property company. A point worth noting is that at this particular time, the world was going through a global financial crisis, and Ireland was experiencing a major property crash and economic turmoil, and as a result, property companies were making redundancies and cutting salaries. Our company was no different, and all of the staff over the past few months had to accept that the financial rewards for working for the company moving forward, would be reduced, which I knew would have a major impact on my livelihood.

I started to go through a range of emotions, and going to work each day was becoming more of a struggle than I had liked. I was trying to manage my MS symptoms as best as possible and I was also working out what was the best path to take for my career. I was in the comfort zone at work and felt that I really needed to move on if I was to develop as a professional, blossom as an entrepreneur, and increase my standing financially. Through the personal development work I had embraced, I was starting to work out that if you are not happy with your financial position or your career, then it's up to you to take control and make the changes required.

In July 2010, I informed my company that I was leaving, handed back the company car, and the hardest of all, handed back the company credit card. I was going to set up my own company and work for myself. I always had regarded myself as an entrepreneur, and this was my big chance to talk the talk and walk the walk. Most people I spoke with thought I was completely crazy, as we were going through one of the worst property crashes of all time, the economy was in recession, and the other small thing—yeah I had a potentially very debilitating condition in MS. In hindsight, I do recognize that it was a very bullish move; however, it was a defining point in my life for all the right reasons.

Life is all about decisions: making enough right decisions and limiting the wrong decisions. I was quite fortunate that Kate always had been extremely supportive of my decisions, and I also benefitted from the advice of a couple of excellent business mentors who I have been able to call upon at any time.

My consultancy business opened its doors in September 2010, and thankfully, to this day, it is going from strength to strength. I went from an office of over one hundred people to an office of one, and I won't lie; it was very difficult, especially those first six months, but I was thriving on the pressure. It was not as if I needed this sort of disruption and challenge in my life, but my gut was telling me that I had to make that tough decision for both my family and myself.

The other small thing that was going on throughout the summer of 2010 was that my beautiful wife was pregnant with our first baby. This was an unbelievable feeling, and as the baby was due in September, I was overjoyed with anticipation and excitement. What made this even more special was that when I first got sick, one of my major concerns was that maybe Kate and I would never have children. Twelve months later when I was diagnosed, these fears were made more real as I had thought that as I now had MS there was little chance of us having a family. Fast forward thirty-six months, and Kate was pregnant and I was going to be a daddy, which was a tremendous feeling.

My MS symptoms were settling throughout 2010, and my coping mechanisms had adjusted a lot better to the situation. I was exercising and training hard, my diet was good, I was taking my Copaxone every day, I had left my job and started my own business, and lastly, Kate was expecting our baby. I was pretty busy, but man had I got my zest back for life. Over the course of the past twelve months since I made a decision to get better and decided to have a super life, my life took a turn for the better, and that was tremendous. The astonishing thing about this was the overall improvement in my life—both physically and mentally—coincided with my twelve-month plan to tackle my problems head on.

At 1:15 a.m. on 28 September 2010, Lilyanna Devine was born in Antrim hospital, Northern Ireland. Kate was fantastic throughout the pregnancy, and although she had an emergency caesarean section, she was extremely strong, and this little ball of fun was handed to me weighing in at seven pounds and two ounces. As I looked at her little face, I was just completely overjoyed. I held Kate's hand throughout the delivery, and now I had the little princess in my life. I was full of emotion and felt my life was now complete.

As I drove home from the hospital at 3:30 a.m. that morning, I found myself reflecting on my life to date and thoughts of what the future may hold. It was four years since my life had changed forever on a beach in Mauritius. The first two years can only be described as a complete disaster in every form of the word. In the last twelve months, I had felt that I had completely changed things around on a mammoth scale. I was winning my MS battle, I had my own business that was going well, my marriage was strong, my faith in god was strong, and I now had a little daughter to complete my family. As I lay in bed that night with these thoughts dancing through my mind, I asked god how it had all turned around for the good. How could someone go from a place so low to a place full of opportunity and possibilities in forty-eight months. As I lay there with these beautiful thoughts, I heard the little positive man on my shoulder whisper the answer: "Conor, this has all happened for one reason—you believed it was possible, you had faith in yourself, faith in god, and you never gave up even in the darkest of times. Your attitude defines you in life and your attitude is fantastic." I literally heard this voice talking to me in this way, and that's what I want to share with you.

If you have the right attitude, you can achieve anything you want. If you apply the right attitude to your marriage, I believe you will have a successful marriage, in most cases. If you apply the right attitude to your work, I believe your achievements from a professional capacity will be endless. If you have the right attitude towards your illness, I know and believe that it is possible to reverse your symptoms and win the battle. Attitude is that small little thing that if you change or tweak it, you can make a massive difference to your circumstances. That's what I believe, and my own personal experience tells me I am correct in my analysis.

Let me ask you some questions—

Have you ever blamed another person or a circumstance for your lack of success?

Have you felt like you couldn't make more money because you didn't have the education or the tools?

Have you felt like you couldn't lose weight because your family has poor genetics?

Have you ever felt that you weren't succeeding because others had been given an unfair advantage?

The truth is that we have all felt these things at one time or another—myself included—and the reality is that as long as you continue to stay in negative mode, your progress will be very limited.

In order to progress in life, we need to take one hundred percent responsibility for our actions and decisions. Daily, in all areas of our lives from our waistline to our bank account, from our relationships to our career, the reality is that in order to be successful we must fully surrender to the notion that we, and we alone, are responsible for creating what we want in our lives. If you apply the wrong attitude to the various aspects of your life, you will get poor results in all areas. If you apply the right attitude, you will reap the benefits in all areas of your life. Life is full of choices, and I chose to apply the right attitude to my life and my illness and am now reaping the benefits on all fronts.

On reflection, I now understand that the first two and a half years of my MS, I admit, that I did not take responsibility. I blamed the MS diagnosis on everything I could think of. I used MS as a reason not to do things and as an excuse to blame myself if I failed. When my financial situation deteriorated, I blamed my employer for not paying me enough, and of course, this was wrong. I now accept that my lack of responsibility and poor attitude contributed to my circumstances in every sense—including the severity of my MS.

When we want to be successful, we have to take responsibility; it is the only way. This means admitting mistakes, letting go of blaming others, and standing tall if we know we have done our best. I meet people every day who blame everyone else for their problems, and I used to be one of those people to a certain extent. Unless you change your attitude you are going to stay in that place of hardship until you accept that you have not only attracted the life you are living but that you are creating even more hardship by refusing to accept that no one else is responsible for your challenges or your successes except you.

It is easy to be angry, judgmental, and even spiteful. When we are in this place, we are attracting more anger, judgment, and spite toward ourselves. The true liberation comes with being able to be compassionate with others, and thus more compassionate with ourselves. Who in your life deserves an apology? Who have you been blaming for your lack of success? Are they really responsible? Or are they, just like you, doing the best they can?

I want to encourage you to own your life and take full responsibility. Let go of the judgment, justification, and jealousy, and truly embrace the fact that attitude is everything. I now believe that you can have what you want to have. Please consider what I refer to as my *three golden rules*, and think about rolling them into your own plan:

1. Make A Decision

   Whatever you wish for in life, the starting point is to make a decision. I made a decision in 2009, that I was going to beat this MS and then went about acting on this decision. If you cannot make a decision, you will not make progress.

2. Take Action

   If you made that decision, well done. The next stage is that you have to act on it. If you have been blaming someone else for your lack of success or poor health—STOP! Instead, take control of the situation by taking control of your mind and taking action. Stop the negativity, pull together a strategic plan that will assist you getting back to the program, and stick to it. Study your illness or challenge, and get around positive people as this type of energy is contagious and its good food for your brain.

3. Belief

   It is no good having a fantastic attitude, making a decision, and taking action if you do not believe one hundred percent that it will work. I now accept that even in my darkest hours of my MS symptoms, the little positive guy on my shoulder kept whispering to me to never give up. Too many times the little negative man drowned him out, but all along, this voice kept encouraging me to believe that anything was possible. Belief is definitely one of the more difficult traits to develop, but daily personal development and commitment to your plan, will help you develop the belief you need.

Reality is the mirror of your thoughts. Choose well what you put in front of the mirror.

ANONYMOUS

CHAPTER 6   OPERATION 26.2

I t was a bright, frisky September morning in 2010, and I was driving to work in Belfast when my phone rang. It was Ann Walker from Action MS, one of the leading Northern Ireland charity organizations for multiple sclerosis. Ann is a great lady who was diagnosed with MS over thirty-five years ago. After a short time considering what to do with her life post-diagnosis, she made a decision to devote herself to helping other people with MS. Thirty-five years on, she is Chairwomen of the charity she founded, and on a daily basis her organization is working to help people with the condition and raise awareness through various campaigns across the country.

Me: "So how is the form today. Ann?"

Ann: "Great, Conor, what about you?"

Me: "Yes I am in good form, Ann."

Ann: "Conor, I want to ask you, and you don't have to say yes; would you be interested in going on a television program to raise awareness for MS and help us raise some funds?"

(Few second pause)

I've always been interested in television and in my early years appeared in a number of dramas and plays and at one time, a career in TV was what I wanted to do. This was possibly my big chance.

Me: "That's no problem, Ann—so, what's going on, what is it all about?"

Ann: "Well the only thing is, Conor, you would have to be willing to run the Belfast Marathon in May 2011, which is eight months away—what do you think?"

In a heartbeat, I accepted the challenge.

Me: "So how do I take this forward Ann?"

Ann: "Ok we have entered you into a local radio station competition, which has asked for people with underlying health problems to enter, from which they would select ten people who they felt had an interesting story to share with the public. As you have a great story and are an inspiration to many—especially the young—I think you would be terrific. What do you think?"

Conor: "No problem Ann, I'll do it."

That week I entered the competition, and sure enough, six weeks later, and after two interviews with the producer of the program, I was selected to take part in the television show that would be going out under the name of *Going the Distance* across BBC1 in Northern Ireland during the following spring.

I was now just over three years post diagnosis, and my plan to get back to a healthy state of mind and body was well under way. I was back training at the gym regularly, my diet was good, and I was reading a lot of personal development material that was helping me get into a good place—both mentally and physically. My thinking on the TV appearance was that first, it was a great challenge that would allow me to help raise some cash for Action MS; secondly, I could raise a lot of awareness of multiple sclerosis throughout the country; thirdly, I might end up inspiring other people with illnesses to fight back against their own conditions. I was very excited about the program, and Kate thought I should definitely get involved, so I couldn't wait for it to get started.

The training started in November 2010 when I met up with the rest of the group for the first time. We had a mixed group in terms of health problems: cancer recovery patients, diabetics, and some with obesity issues, amongst other problems. We all underwent full medicals and were assigned personal trainers to get us ready for the big day that was just a few months away. For those of you who don't know much about marathons, it's a road race that totals 26.2 miles.

The Belfast course is quite hilly and recognized as one of the more difficult marathons to take part in across Europe. Although I was back training and getting a little fitter, the thought of running 26.2 miles in a few months was seriously daunting. Five, maybe ten, miles I could handle, but a marathon—that was something else. I actually detested long distance running, but very quickly, I needed to get my head right and start planning for the challenge, which is exactly what I did.

Over the next few months, the cast of the show trained together every few weeks and the film crew were with us quite a bit. They also visited us at home for interviews that would be screened during the show around April 2011—a few weeks before the race. The idea was there would be eight thirty-minute shows and a likely audience of approximately 250,000 viewers. The thought of the whole project started to get exciting, and I was really focusing now, as my goals for getting involved were very clear and achievable.

When training for a marathon, you have to be very structured in terms of your training runs and your diet. We started out with the shorter runs of four to five miles, and then built up over the following few months to twelve and fifteen-mile runs. One thing about me over the years is that I have developed a very strong mind-set. Generally, if I put my mind to something, I will do it, and as for this challenge, it would be no different. I knew that if I trained hard enough, and my MS symptoms were kept under control, come May 2011, I would have run my first marathon.

I was starting to get really into the whole challenge, and it was great getting to know the other people who were on the show. Everyone in the group found the whole project very difficult, and the training days when we congregated were quite testing. What made matters worse was the weather in Ireland during mid-winter time is pretty poor, so marathon training is not the most fantastic thing you could be spending your time doing. I was attending the local gym three times a week and had personal training sessions twice a month. I usually tried to get my training done in the morning time as it meant it had less impact on my job. After a few months, I could feel my body getting into better condition and my MS symptoms were under control. I was still experiencing daily symptoms, but since I implemented a plan to fight the MS, I certainly was seeing a vast improvement in my overall health condition.

For the first time since my diagnosis, I started to feel as if I was beating MS and was more determined than ever to keep persevering and spreading the message that if I could do this, you could too. It wasn't that long ago that I had accepted in the not-too-distant future that I might be in a wheelchair and just existing. Fast forward eighteen months, and I am preparing for my first marathon challenge and in control of my symptoms—the feeling was incredible. Walking through a supermarket was a tough challenge a couple of years back, but I was starting to accept that I really was making superb progress. My mind was getting stronger, my attitude was good, and I was getting my confidence back. I truly believed that if other people with MS saw the TV show and saw me crossing the finish line, it would give them a lot of hope that they too might be able to improve if they implemented the right plan.

When I started my fight for recovery, I remembered reading where Montel Williams was advocating to test yourself, set goals, and to take control of your life. He was saying that you can still lead a full life, and that the secret was really to develop the right attitude. If you can do this, you will see life change for the good. I was now experiencing this, and the feeling inside me was fantastic.

It was mid February 2011, and the television program makers decided it'd be a great idea as part of our training for us to enter the Larne Half Marathon, which would be our first big test. As we had little choice in the matter, all we could do was prepare properly in January and hope we would be fine on the day. We arrived on the Saturday morning, did our usual TV interviews pre-race, and shortly after that, we were on our way. Out of the full group taking part in the show, it was clear from the first day on the training track that I was the fittest of everyone, probably due to the fact that I was the youngest and came from a sporting background. This wasn't important, but what the other cast members didn't have was the handicap of having MS symptoms and living with them every day.

On a number of occasions over the training period when we were all just having a chat, many of the other cast members found it hard to understand how I even had MS due to the fact I looked great and was quite fit. Out of all the symptoms and circumstances surrounding the condition, this is one of the most frustrating and difficult points to explain to people, and those of you with the condition will likely agree with me on this one. What you need to understand is that many people with MS look good on the outside because the problem lies within the central nervous system, the body's engine—under the skin.

People with MS have serious problems with their nervous system, which to be frank can cause all sorts of issues throughout the body. It is a silent and in too many cases, a progressive condition that over time can just wear you down in quite a nasty way and make those affected live extremely difficult and miserable lives. There have been times even recently when I have explained that I suffer from MS in general conversation to someone I've just met and the person says,

"You couldn't have…no way."Yes way; I have been diagnosed over six years now and fighting every day against it. After a further explanation (and only then) will most people say, "Flipping heck, I would never have guessed, Conor, you look so well; I really am very sorry to hear that." Therefore, the lesson here is just because someone looks well on the outside, doesn't always necessarily mean they are very healthy and all is ok on the inside.

I crossed the finish line in Larne clocking two hours and twenty-one minutes and was pretty exhausted. It was a tough course with too many hills for my liking, but I had a great sense of achievement when passing through the finish line of my first road race. I was the first of the group home, and over the next while, everyone else got back in one piece. I really enjoyed my first big test and drove home in the car all proud of myself to inform Kate and Lilyanna of my achievement, of which they were delighted and very proud.

Home life was now really rewarding, and Kate had adapted to motherhood like a duck to water and little Lilyanna was an absolute dream. Business was going well and to say my life was busy was an understatement; but to be honest, I wouldn't have had it any other way.

There was about eight weeks to marathon day and my life revolved around training, working, and family time. I was getting up at 6:00 a.m. in the morning and going to the gym three times a week, trying to get a couple of runs in during the evening times and a long run at the weekend. Life was good, and it was such a difference and long distant memory from those early days when my illness had hit nearly four years ago and I was at rock bottom. Don't get me wrong, I still had symptoms most days, but I was certainly in control of things, and my life was now designed around my positive approach and what I wanted to do.

Bank holiday, Monday, 2 May 2011, arrived and I got up early to get some food into my body, as I needed it due to operation 26.2-mile road race a short time later. The crew all met at a hotel in Belfast City centre and everyone was really excited about the day ahead. Thirty thousand people had entered the marathon this year, but we were the only ones with a film crew running after us. I agreed to run with a guy named Michael who I'd become friendly with during the training process. Michael was a local entrepreneur and a health and fitness guru who had a number of marathons and road races under his belt. He had been giving me lots of advice over the past few months and I enjoyed his company and wealth of knowledge in this arena, so it was a real boost when he decided to run with me.

In addition, I had managed to talk twenty-five other friends and family into running in relay teams to raise awareness and money for Action MS. Amazingly, everyone had turned up and it made the whole day absolutely fantastic.

The horn sounded, and the 2011 Belfast marathon began with me in terrific form. The extra special thing again about the day was that Kate was running a leg of the relay and she ran the first six miles with me, which was great. There were smiles and happy faces everywhere, and the best thing of all; we had an absolutely cracking day weather wise—if I dare say even a little on the hot side, which is a rarity in this part of the world.

The first ten miles were great and I was feeling good and very confident about the remainder of the race. At mile fourteen, I stopped to do a short interview with the film crew; then off I went, hoping to stay strong and get home as quick as possible. As this was my first marathon, I wasn't overly concerned about a time, and as I didn't know what to expect, I just wanted to get around in one piece and give it my best shot. Mile sixteen and seventeen started to get very tough. My knees were beginning to ache and my hips were playing up. When we hit the twenty-mile mark, I was starting to struggle even more and would have loved to walk for a while, but Michael encouraged me to keep going, which I did.

One of my regrets in terms of my training was that I didn't do enough long runs. The furthest I had run in training was eighteen miles, and the experts would advise you to do a twenty, and maybe a twenty-two mile. As I hadn't done this, I was now starting to pay for it, and the pain was starting to get very uncomfortable. As I passed the twenty-four-mile marker, every bone in my body was aching and my hips were on fire. Michael was great as he encouraged me to dig in and was a real source of support, especially over the last few miles.

The crowds were fantastic and really drove us on, but the pain was increasing by the second. We hit the twenty-five-mile marker with only just over a mile to go and I was in bits. My legs were now like jelly and I was becoming light headed. I spotted an old football mate of mine in the crowd close to the finish line, the legendary former Liverpool, Fulham and Dungannon Swifts midfielder Rodney Mc Aree, whom I had the pleasure of playing with a couple of years before. He handed me a sports drink, probably with good intentions, but unfortunately after a few swallows, it seemed to have the opposite effect, as I spewed it all down my front, which was a delightful sight—NOT. The lack of energy mixed with the fierce heat was completely pulverizing me at this point and I wanted the finish line.

As we turned in to the last half-mile, I got this brainwave that we should try and make a sprint finish. You know what the Africans do in the Olympic Games. Yes, well, that's what Michael and I decided to do a few hundred yards from the line. The only thing I must point out at this juncture is that I am not an African marathon runner in any shape or form and probably shouldn't have executed this bright idea. I crossed the line with a time of four hours and thirty-four minutes with mixed feelings. In a way, I felt absolutely overjoyed with a sense of achievement and exhilaration; however, in other ways, I thought my head was going to explode into millions of pieces.

My sprint finish idea was probably one of the worst ideas I've ever had in my life, and some forty-five minutes later, I was only starting to come round and enjoy the actual achievement. I was the first one home from the group and it was extra special as my mum, dad, wife, daughter, and lots of other friends and family members where there to welcome me across the line.

I committed to the TV program six months ago and the project was now over. The whole experience was fantastic and I had smashed the goals I set out to achieve. All in, I raised over ten thousand pounds for Action MS, I had spread a very positive message in relation to multiple sclerosis, and I hoped in the months ahead, others might be inspired by my story. I was delighted with how every-thing had gone over the past few months. I always knew deep in my heart that I was a fighter, and that I would win the battle; Today was the day that I started to finally accept and believe that I was beating MS and that I would continue to beat it and lead a fantastic life from that day forward.

"Whatever the mind can conceive and believe, it can achieve." Napoleon Hill

CHAPTER 7   FIND AN INSPIRATION

I never thought I would have been able to say this; however, very proudly, I now accept my multiple sclerosis diagnosis. The one thing that I would say has come about as a very positive result of this experience is that over the past six years, I have really gotten to know myself on a level that I never really thought was possible. Being diagnosed with such a showstopper of an illness is a challenge that requires a champion Olympian reaction. Anyone who succeeds in the battle against such an illness is no less a hero in my book than the person who wins a gold medal at the Olympic Games. You may not get a place on a podium and the national anthem played, but the prize is much better than any gold medal: You get your life back.

When faced with adversity and illness, you can either sink or swim—as there is no hiding place. For two and a half years, I was sinking very quickly into a small dark hole. I couldn't see or work out how I was going to fight the MS, have a career, and be a loving husband and father. I only had questions and very little answers. As every day passed in the early days, I had more and more questions and became completely disillusioned with life and why I was even on this earth. Apart from the physical difficulties an MS diagnosis brings with it, it's also one lonely journey; despite the best intentions of family and friends, ultimately the buck stops with you. I was very fortunate that I have a fantastic family and an incredible wife, but I have no problem admitting that at one time, I just didn't think I was going to come out the other side. You go through all sorts of emotions, from fear to anger, regret to pity, anxiety, hopelessness, dismay, and disappointment. I've been through all of these ten times over multiplied by one hundred thousand. However, it is ok to have all of these feelings. In fact, I would suggest if you have just been diagnosed with a condition or have been sick for quite a while, if you haven't felt any of the emotions you are not normal, so its ok, trust me.

It took me twenty-eight years to come to understand that life is not straightforward. I believe that every single one of us hits a wall in life, and when you hit that wall, you have some choices to make. I now know that I hit my wall completely unexpectedly at twenty-eight years old, and for three years, I found it extremely tough. What you need to understand is it's not the falling down that matters — it's the staying down that causes the long-term problems. That's where I would encourage you to change from this day forward.

One of the ways I've learned to cope with my condition is that I now know that I am in a very privileged place with my life, and the reality is that there are millions of people a hell of a lot worse off than me.

I have a good friend called Trevor who lives not too far from me, and he is one of my true inspirations in life. He runs a very successful business and is a major employer in the area. Just over five years ago, Trevor, a motorbike enthusiast, had a very bad accident and drove straight into a concrete post at over one hundred miles per hour. He ended up in a coma for three months and the outlook for him was not good. He had a loving wife and four children at home, and his whole family was absolutely devastated and sick with worry of what the future held for them all. One day, Trevor opened his eyes in the intensive care unit and decided to start the very long, difficult fight back to some form of normality and health. The tragic result of his accident was that Trevor had badly damaged his spinal cord, and as a result, he couldn't move his body from the waist down.

Over the last few years, Trevor has continued to fight pain and all sorts of daily challenges that come with being confined to a wheelchair. His love for his family and never-say-die attitude is nothing short of inspirational and amazing. He has gone through dozens of operations and is trawling the world for stem cell treatment that just might allow him to walk again one day. He is at his desk each morning at 8:30 a.m. and running a multi-million pound company. He is nothing short of remarkable and his courage is incredible.

Trevor doesn't know this, but when I was getting things very tough, I drew inspiration from him in the fight he has shown to get up and embrace the challenges he faces every day. He is in different degrees of pain twenty-four hours a day, and I just pray that someday soon he gets a little rest and finds a breakthrough that will help him and ease his pain.

I am sharing this story with you because every single one of us knows someone like Trevor. We all know many people who are struggling financially, or in their marriage, or struggling through illness or bereavement. We all hit the wall at some point in our lives, but it's important to realize when you are down on the floor that there are many people in a similar position, if not a lot worse. I am not saying this makes things for you any easier; however, for me it definitely put things into perspective and I draw strength from people like Trevor.

If you know of anyone who is in a difficult spot and yet is fighting through it every day, compliment that person and try to draw strength from him or her, and then put a plan in place that will pull you out of your own dark place. I now believe that absolutely everything is possible, but you have to have the desire, motivation, and willpower to fire your engines.

When I look back at some of the difficult periods I went through in the first twelve months of my diagnosis, I realize that I was so upset with how ill I was that I couldn't even shed a tear. I now know that this was all part of the process and part of the acceptance of my condition. Yes, being diagnosed with multiple sclerosis at twenty-eight years old was one hell of a kick in the teeth. I was planning for world domination with my business ideas, about to marry my childhood sweetheart, and then all of a sudden *Bang*; my dreams are in tatters.

I mean this when I say this: my MS diagnosis has defined me as the person I always wanted to be. It has helped me understand who I actually am, and has helped me get to where I've wanted to get to.

Today, I have more goals set to achieve that I never would have thought possible. From a business point of view, I have made incredible progress in the past twenty-four months, and the next thirty-six months look to be extremely exciting. From a health perspective, I am now setting and smashing goals that I never would have dreamed off, and I am convinced that I never would have experienced them if I hadn't hit my wall. In a funny sort of way, I have a lot to thank my MS diagnosis for, and I do not say that lightly. There have been so many times, and I still get these moments, whereby that little negative man on my shoulder is sitting whispering into my ear, "Conor, just give up; you will never do this." Well, do you know how wrong he is? I will always persevere to achieve and smash my goals.

My family is very important to me, and my mum is one in a million. She has a great personality and from a young age both her and dad couldn't do enough for all the children. It was a pleasure growing up in our household, and I am very grateful for the environment my parents created.

When I was very young, my mum always encouraged me to be the best that I could be. I remember when I was about ten or eleven and my mum used to tell me that I was a fantastic footballer and could achieve anything if I put my mind to. She always encouraged me and built me up, making me feel ten feet tall. It's amazing now, looking back after over twenty years, how I can vividly remember some of the positive comments she made to me in our kitchen and living room at our home in Cookstown. When I was getting it really tight in the early years of diagnosis, those positive comments my mum used to say to me came back into my mind in my hour of need and encouraged and challenged me to fight back and never give up. This may be worth noting if you are a parent: remember to encourage your kids as much as possible. Build them up, as there will be people queuing up to knock them down throughout their own lives.

I now try every single day to be as positive as I can be and the best I can be. This is not always easy as there are times when I get it pretty tight, am quite down, and it's hard to be positive. At times, my symptoms can be difficult, and the negative dark cloud attempts to take over my mind. One of the things I find that helps me get back on track is to read a good book. Through my MS diagnosis, and subsequent search for on-going personal development and achievement, I have read many books and publications that have helped me develop in many ways. I find that if I stop reading for a few weeks, negativity can set in and I start to lose my focus. When this happens now, I tend to pick up a book—or more recently my Kindle—and get stuck into it. This gets me back on track, and reading has become a major part of my down time, and my life.

Through my personal development and search for improvement as a person, I feel this has really helped me beat the MS. Your mental health is extremely important, and it is important that we all look after ourselves in this regard. MS patients really struggle with this whole area in particular. I find through my exercise regime, diet, and positive approach to life that I have a very good basis of mental health. I firmly believe that my exercise regime has helped me immensely in my fight with MS. I am now probably the fittest I have ever been and running and competing in marathons and other events is part of my life. I am incredibly proud now when I finish a race because I know I can inspire people to believe in themselves more, and also I continue to prove the medical experts wrong. I can show them that getting a MS diagnosis doesn't mean that you will end up in a wheelchair as I had thought when I was first diagnosed.

In addition to being essential to general health and well-being, it is widely accepted exercise is helpful in managing many MS symptoms. A study published by researchers at the University of Utah in 1996 was the first to demonstrate clearly the benefits of exercise for people with MS. Those patients who participated in an aerobic exercise program had better cardiovascular fitness, improved strength, better bladder and bowel function, less fatigue and depression, a more positive attitude, and increased participation in social activities. Since 1996, several additional studies have confirmed the benefits of exercise.

Inactivity in people with or without MS can result in numerous risk factors associated with coronary heart disease. In addition, it can lead to weakness of muscles, decreased bone density with an increased risk of fracture, and shallow, inefficient breathing.

I would like to caveat that any exercise program needs to be appropriate to the capabilities and limitations of the individual, and may need to be adjusted as changes occur in MS symptoms. My advice is to be careful and consult your physiotherapist; they will be helpful in designing, supervising, and revising a well-balanced exercise program. Remember, you should advise your GP and neurologist of your physical exertions, as they will want to keep a record of your progress.

A good exercise program can help to develop the maximum potential of muscle, bone, and respiration, thereby avoiding secondary complications and gaining the benefits of good health and well-being. Exercise is great, but just be careful and do not overdo things, as it could be more harmful and bring on a relapse, which obviously no one wants.

Have a think about the people in your area who you know are fighting illness. Go and have a chat with them and ask them how they are keeping. There are some remarkable fighters everywhere in society—true champions who are all inspirations in their own right. Draw strength and take note of how they fight their daily battles, and then implement some of their strengths and qualities into your daily routine. Believe me, it works.

Will Smith is a very famous American actor and he is someone who I really admire from a professional point of view. He advocates dreaming, setting, and achieving goals. Through the power of the Internet, you are only a touch of a button away from inspirational people who have fought their own battles to rise to the top. I would encourage you to look these people up, carry out your own research, and draw strength from their experiences.

There is guy called Nick Vucevic who I would encourage you to have a look at. He has no arms, no legs, and his life is incredibly difficult. He is now a very famous motivational speaker who travels the globe speaking to thousands of people, encouraging them to be grateful, to fight back, and believe in themselves. You do not have to be a very accomplished public speaker to fight back and encourage others to believe in themselves. I happen to believe that we can all fight back and we can all inspire at least one other person to believe in him or herself. If everyone in the world did this, wouldn't the world be a much better place? I think so. So get cracking and find at least one person who inspires you. They are out there.

With the right attitude, you can achieve anything.
—— CONOR DEVINE

CHAPTER 8   HOW I BEAT MS

If you find yourself in a difficult situation, the only way you will get out of it is to put a plan in place and follow through with the actions required. One of my main motivations for sharing my story with you is that I now know that through my experience with MS, others will look at it and think to themselves—*Well if he can do it, so can I.* This is a major motivation for me and looking back, I only started to win my MS battle when I came across people like Motel Williams, who shared with me through his books and his own experience that you can fight back and beat the condition. Once you program this in your mind, it is an incredibly powerful tool to fight against anything and put you on your road to recovery.

I developed a plan to help me fight and win this battle, which I put into place almost three years ago. I have talked about the various ingredients that have helped me get to a good place in various chapters of this book, but I have now detailed it below for you to consider in greater detail. This three-point plan is one that has worked for me, and I am only too delighted to share it with you.

INGREDIENTS THAT HAVE HELPED ME BEAT MULTIPLE SCLEROSIS

1.   Medication

If you have just been diagnosed with multiple sclerosis, my very clear view is that you need to get on a course of disease modifying drugs as soon as is physically possible. I must stress at this point that I am not a doctor, but I am qualified to have an opinion on this matter through my own personal experience. Disease modifying drugs are a group of compounds that alter the progression of multiple sclerosis. They have been shown to reduce the frequency and severity of relapses and slow the development of disability in some people.

There are generally three types of disease modifying drugs (DMDs) used in the treatment of MS. These are:

- Beta interferon - which comes in two forms: Beta interferon 1a and Beta interferon 1b

- Glatiramer acetate (Copaxone)

- Tysabri (Natalizumab)

Beta Interferon

Interferons are proteins produced naturally by the human body. They are released by white blood cells to alter the immune system's response to infections.

Gamma interferons, which are released at the start of an immune response to infection, can induce multiple sclerosis symptoms. Beta interferons (sometimes referred to as interferon beta) are known to block the action of gamma interferons. It is thought that beta interferons act by reducing both inflammation and the body's autoimmune reaction that is responsible for the destruction of myelin.

There are four beta interferon drugs available and it is vital that you take the advice of your neurologist when deciding which form to run with.

When I was diagnosed in 2007, my neurologist and I talked through the options I had for medication and recommended I try Beta Interferon. Over the course of the next six months, my symptoms actually got worse as the drug did not agree with my body so I came off it immediately.

Glatiramer acetate (Copaxone)

Glatiramer acetate, better known as Copaxone, is one of the disease modifying drugs licensed for relapsing remitting multiple sclerosis. Studies have shown that on average, Copaxone reduces the MS relapse rate by about a third. This drug is a synthetic combination of four amino acids, resembling the myelin protein surrounding nerve fibers. It is thought to lessen the immune reaction that attacks myelin.

After my bad experience with the beta interferon, my neurologist recommended I get on Copaxone straight away. Thankfully, there were no side effects to this drug for me and I have been injecting fifty milliliters every day for the past five and a half years. Yes, I still do not like needles, but I've taken the view that if this little potion can help me stay strong in the long run, I will keep taking it.

Tysabri

Tysabri, also known as Natalizumab, is a disease-modifying drug licensed for use with people with highly active relapsing remitting multiple sclerosis (two or more disabling relapses in one year). Studies have shown that Tysabri reduces the occurrence of relapse by around two thirds and significantly reduces the rate of disease progression.

Tysabri is a type of drug called monoclonal antibodies. It binds to molecules on the surface of specific immune cells and it is thought to act by preventing the cells from passing into the central nervous system via the blood-brain barrier.

It is one of the more user-friendly drugs in terms of the way it is administered as it is taken as an intravenous (IV) infusion via a drip once every four weeks.

When I was having a bad experience with Rebiff my neurologist and I discussed Tysabri; however, we both agreed that we would give Copaxone a go, and thankfully, to date that decision has proved correct.

Disease modifying drugs are not a cure for MS, but they can reduce the frequency of relapses. Scientists don't yet know whether any of these drugs will slow down the rate of disability in the long term. In this day and age, the advances in the medical world are phenomenal, and the advances in MS Research in the past few years have also been fantastic. A number of disease modifying drugs are available on the marketplace, and over the next few years, drugs that are more effective will be available once the results of their trials come to a close. Copaxone is my drug of choice and it seems to be working very well for me. There are little to no side effects with the only downside being you have to inject yourself every morning, but you get used to that part.

Last month, I went to see my neurologist, whom I hadn't seen in over two years, and he was amazed by my progress. I had run the idea past him that I might stop the medication as I thought I maybe didn't need it anymore. He immediately nipped this in the bud and told me that this was not one of my better ideas, and I would be crazy to stop something after the rate of progress I had experienced. One thing I wouldn't put me down for is being stupid, and Dr. Watt is a very clever man; so, I won't be stopping my medication, nor would I advise anyone to do the same.

My advice is to make sure you get on the right medication, though, and this will certainly help you in my opinion. Remember, I am not a medical professional in any way—I'm just a MS Champion. Please take the appropriate medical advice when coming to such an important decision.

2.   Diet and Exercise

<u>Diet</u>

General diet recommendations

From when I was a young boy, I have always had a fairly balanced diet. When I say this, I mean that I ate most things that my mother put in front of me to include lots of fruit and vegetables. I remember my mum always use to say to me that eating carrots would help improve my eyesight. As a result, I use to over load on the carrots at any chance I got, and guess what? Today I have twenty-twenty vision. Now, please take this with a pinch of salt, but as far as I'm concerned; the carrots definitely helped in development of my great eyesight – Thanks mum.

All joking aside, of all the recommended strategies for fighting disease and promoting overall health and well-being, few are as critical and profound as the practice of healthy eating. Over the last few years, I have come to understand that healthy eating is a lifelong process of nourishing our bodies, minds, and spirits. However, it is not about depriving ourselves completely of foods that we enjoy. Even when a specific medical condition dictates such restriction, a number of healthier alternatives to our favorite foods are available on the market.

I happen to believe that healthy eating ought to be viewed as the regular consumption of a wide variety of nourishing, whole foods accompanied by positive attitudes toward eating wholesome meals that together, provide us with the ability to rejuvenate and rebuild. It is not easy, and it does require a certain amount of discipline and planning. However, whether you suffer from MS, another illness, or maybe you do not have any form of illness at all, it is generally accepted worldwide that your diet plays a key role in life expectancy and quality of life you will have.

There is overwhelming evidence that supports an organic, whole foods based diet full of a variety of fresh fruits and vegetables as a means to better health.

Due to the high nutritional and antioxidant content of many whole foods, this type of diet is linked with increased antioxidant activity, improved digestion, healthy inflammation response, healthy glucose metabolism, and increased immune activity, among other benefits.

When I talk about whole foods, I am referring to foods that are available in their original form, minimally processed and/or refined, and not containing additives of any kind. Whole foods consist mainly of fresh fruits and vegetables, whole grains (not hulled or polished), and raw nuts and seeds. Animal products should be organic and eaten in smaller quantities. Aside from a higher phytochemical (plant nutrient and antioxidant) profile, whole foods contain much higher amounts of fiber—the regular consumption of which is linked to reduced cancer and heart disease. High fiber diets promote overall gastrointestinal health, as well as the detoxification of toxins and heavy metals.

When I first was hit with MS, and during the next two years of diagnosis, my diet was not top of the agenda, as I hadn't worked out my plan to fight back against the illness. However, as I started to find people who had adopted similar strategies in relation to diet and had seen the positive impact it was making on their lives and their MS, I thought it prudent to consider and follow suit. In the past two and a half years, I certainly have tried to stick as best I can to my new diet, and it is most definitely working: I am winning my MS battle, and I feel so much better overall than I did during those early days of the condition.

In general, I recommend following a whole foods diet as much as possible, focusing on fruits and vegetables that are seasonal and organic.

Nutritional value and good tasting, fulfilling foods are not mutually exclusive. If you are not accustomed to eating non-artificially flavored, unprocessed foods, it may take time for your taste buds, and ultimately, your brain, to appreciate healthier food choices. However, remember not to be too hard on yourself. Guilt and negative feelings towards eating perceived "unhealthy" foods could cause more harm to your health than the actual foods themselves. Healthy eating can easily be an enjoyable part of your lifestyle, and as you continue your dedication to wholesome choices for yourself on every level—body, mind and spirit—your being will reward you with radiant health and a certain inner tranquillity that arises from being truly nourished and fulfilled.

There are now lots of information on MS available through the Internet and books, and I spent days upon days studying and researching as much as I could because I was determined to get back to full health. Many people I came across were saying the same thing: if I modified my lifestyle and my diet, my symptoms may improve.

My view is very clear, and I believe without a doubt that every person with MS should live as healthy a lifestyle as they possibly can. Lifestyle modification is not a cure for MS, but as of right now, neither is the medication; a combination of both is beneficial I would suggest.

MS is a disease that damages the protective fatty myelin sheath that surrounds the nerves in the brain and spinal cord. When the immune system goes into overdrive, it produces an inflammatory response that strips away the myelin and causes nerve scarring. This impairs the transmission of nerve impulses and it's what causes the numerous different symptoms of MS. The central nervous system can sometimes regenerate damaged nerve tissue—but only if there is minimal demyelination. A key way to reduce MS relapses is to reduce the inflammation that causes the demyelination in the first place.

Years have been spent researching holistic nutrition and lifestyle modification for the management of MS, as well as numerous other inflammatory conditions. The results of which concluded the lifestyle someone with MS should follow is the same healthy lifestyle anyone should follow who wants to live long and live well, and this includes adhering to the following basic guidelines:

- Eating a nutrient-dense and anti-inflammatory diet based on unrefined whole foods with an emphasis on plant-based foods (fruits, vegetables, beans, whole grains, nuts, seeds, etc.) and a de-emphasis on land-animal foods (beef, chicken, eggs, dairy, etc.).

- Significantly reducing saturated fat from animal foods and eliminating Tran's fats (these fats are thought to stimulate the Th1 response—the release of myelin-damaging inflammatory chemicals by immune cells).

- Increasing intake of omega-3 fats from seafood and vegan sources (particularly flax and chia seeds).

- Stress management

- Nutritional supplements (specifically with omega-3 essential fats and vitamin D-3).

Managing Your Symptoms with Your Diet

The purpose of dietary modification for the management of MS is multifactorial:

1) Anyone with any autoimmune related disease should consume as many nutrient-dense calories and as few empty calories as possible in order for the immune system to have the best chance of functioning at its most efficient. Specific to MS: a broad spectrum of nutrients is essential in order for the brain to repair itself.

2) MS is a disease made worse by inflammation—the immune system has different ways it can damage the brain and there are major variations in the amount of damage inflammation causes. Each time you have an exacerbation or flare-up, the inflammation that occurs has the potential to cause debilitating symptoms. Yet by modifying the foods you eat

to include more anti-inflammatory foods and fewer pro-inflammatory foods, you can help prevent the inflammatory flare-ups that cause MS symptoms. You are not "curing" MS with diet; you are simply controlling the symptoms and helping to prevent future damage.

3) Eating a nutrient-dense and anti-inflammatory diet is also the best diet for weight management, and maintaining a healthy bodyweight makes living with MS much easier. Additionally, it is important to avoid overeating excessive amounts of empty calories as doing so can put the body's inflammatory process into overdrive.

4) Getting the proper nutrition and avoiding empty calories is essential for having energy and combating the overwhelming fatigue so many MS patients find debilitating.

Whenever you are diagnosed with an illness, it's important that you give yourself every chance to fight it on a daily basis. Now every morning when I wake up I have a think about what I am going to eat that day and try and design my lifestyle around healthy eating. The food and drink I put into my body gives me the energy to work and play every day. Doesn't it make so much sense that all of us should be a lot more health conscious and sort our diets out, allowing us to have a better longer quality of life?

EXERCISE

Let's be very clear, regular exercise is a good idea for anyone. However, for the estimated 2.5 million people worldwide living with multiple sclerosis, there are benefits that are even more specific.

Interestingly enough, doctors used to recommend that people living with MS avoid exercise entirely due to fear of aggravating symptoms. But now there is a great deal of evidence to suggest that regular exercise not only improves quality of life for people with multiple sclerosis, but that it may also help ease symptoms and minimize the risk of certain complications later in life.

Many MS clinicians have put on record that making exercise "part of a healthy lifestyle, with two or three sessions per week" is a good idea for most people living with MS. There is enough evidence to suggest that specific exercises can help people address particular mobility issues.

My clear advice on this is, before you start any MS exercise program, to be sure to consult your doctor or physician about what type of program is best suited to yourself.

The Benefits of Exercise for MS Patients

Getting active can help relieve a number of symptoms and complications that are commonly associated with MS. These include:

Fatigue

Being extra tired is a common complaint among people with multiple sclerosis. Exercise, including yoga, can help combat this. A recent study examined the fatigue levels of people living with multiple sclerosis; one group signed on for a yoga class geared to the needs of people with MS, a second group took a stationary-bicycling class, and a third group had no specific program given to them. At the end of the six-month study, both the yoga and stationary bike participants reported improvement in their fatigue levels, while the third group, who had no specific exercise program, saw no improvement in their MS fatigue symptoms. I found this very interesting indeed. I have recently added a weekly Pilate's class to my training program and find this very beneficial for my mental and physical health.

Bladder control

In 1996, Jack Petajan, M.D.—a researcher who had multiple sclerosis—conducted one of the pioneering studies on the role of exercise in people living with MS. Dr. Petajan, who died in 2005, found that even moderate to regular exercise helped to correct bladder control issues that are common in people with multiple sclerosis. I found this evidence also very interesting and difficult to ignore.

Stronger bones

Weight-bearing exercise is a good way to strengthen bones and protect against osteoporosis, a bone-thinning disease. People with multiple sclerosis are at particular risk for osteoporosis due to a combination of factors. For one, levels of vitamin D—the nutrient that works with calcium to protect bone health—are typically low among people living with MS. Certain medications (such as corticosteroids) that are effective in the treatment of MS flare-ups can also lead to lower calcium levels. These lower levels of vitamin D and calcium make it harder for your body to retain bone density or strength. At the same time, people with multiple sclerosis often face mobility issues that make them more prone to falling, which can lead to broken bones.

The good news is you can combat these vitamin and mineral deficiencies and further strengthen your bones with exercise. Weight-bearing exercises—including running, aerobics, Pilates, dancing, and stair climbing—help you build and maintain bone density that will protect your bones, even if you stumble and fall.

Weight management

The decrease in mobility caused by multiple sclerosis, combined with the side effects of common MS medications (such as steroid drugs used to treat flare-ups), can lead to weight gain, which can contribute to a further decrease in your ability to get around. Exercise can slow or stop this cycle.

<u>Heart health</u>

Multiple sclerosis may increase the risk of heart problems due to its effect on involuntary bodily processes such as breathing, digestion, and heart rhythm. Staying physically active has long been promoted as a healthy way to decrease risks for heart disease. Even mild or moderate activity can help minimize your risk of cardiovascular problems down the line.

For many people, multiple sclerosis means a change in physical activity and mobility, but it does not mean that life comes to a standstill. If you are unable to continue activities that you used to enjoy, talk to your doctor about new ways to stay active, or talk to a physical therapist about ways to make your old favorite activities more accessible.

<u>Tips for Safe Exercise with Multiple Sclerosis</u>

- Always warm up before beginning your exercise routine, and cool down at the end.

- If you plan to work out for thirty minutes, start with ten-minute work-out sessions and work your way up.

- Workout in a safe environment; avoid slippery floors, poor lighting, throw rugs, and other potential hazards.

- If you have difficulty balancing, exercise within reach of a grab bar or rail.

- If at any time you feel sick or you begin to hurt, STOP.

- Select an activity that you enjoy and have fun! Water aerobics, swimming, tai chi, pilates, and yoga are examples of exercises that often work well for people with MS.

Sport is something that I embraced from a very early age, and as I've explained earlier in this book, I was a very competitive sportsman and played different sports at a decent level. Growing up evolved around playing football and training, so it would be fair to say that I always had a decent level of fitness. When my MS problem hit me at twenty-eight, I stopped everything sport related instantly. The shock of what had happened had blown me apart, and my symptoms were very debilitating, which meant even walking at times was quite difficult.

For a couple of years, my activity levels were low, and my medical team were against me training at the gym or playing football again. During my research into MS, I started to realize that many people worldwide advocated sport and exercise as a way to help the body fight MS.

Life generally is all about decisions we make and the actions we carry out, and just over three years ago, I decided to start an exercise regime with the hope that it would help me in my fight back. Fast forward a few years and I am glad to confirm that exercise is now a major part of my life, and I believe it has played a major role in assisting me win my MS battle. Please accept that I am merely sharing my experience with you however many medics also have put it on record that a medium level of exercise can assist MS patients.

In 2010, I took up running, and I have never looked back. In the last eighteen months, I have run two marathons, two half marathons and many more miles of training runs.

I would encourage anyone who has MS to implement some element of exercise into his or her daily routine. Over a period of time, you should feel your body get a little stronger, and this will give you extra encouragement and confidence. Generally, I would say you will reap the benefits in a very short period of time, and overall the lifestyle benefits are worth investing in.

3.   Positive Mental Attitude

Every day I would guess-timate that I read at least one hundred positive and motivational quotes through social networking sites or books and publications. Applying a very positive approach to my MS condition has equipped me with the artillery that is required to fight such a potentially devastating illness. I have detailed below a flavour of some of the brain food I digest on a daily basis:

- *Always turn a negative situation into a positive situation.* **Michael Jordan**

- *Choosing to be positive and having a grateful attitude is going to determine how you're going to live your life.* **Joel Osteen**

- *People are always blaming their circumstances for what they are. I don't believe in circumstances. The people who get on in this world are the people who get up and look for the circumstances they want, and if they can't find them, make them.* **George Bernard Shaw**

- *The great pleasure in life is doing what people say you cannot do.* **Walter Bagehot**

- *There is one quality that one must possess to win, and that is definiteness of purpose, the knowledge of what one wants, and a burning desire to possess it.* **Napoleon Hill**

- *Too often we underestimate the power of a touch, a smile, a kind word, a listening ear, an honest compliment, or the smallest act of caring, all of which have the potential to turn a life around.* **Leo Buscaglia**

- *The only thing that stands between a man and what he wants from life is often merely the will to try it and the faith to believe that it is possible.* **David Viscott**

- *Experience is not what happens to a man; it is what a man does with what happens to him.* **Huxley, Aldous**

- *If you have the courage to begin, you have the courage to succeed.* **David Viscott**

I never get tired of reading such material, and I will let you in on a secret: I carry a small little red book with me in my car with lots of motivational and positive quotes that I often flick through if I am sitting in traffic or have a few minutes to myself.

Personal development has completely changed my life, and it can change yours, too. However, for this to happen, you really need to apply yourself and be open to change. When I was diagnosed with MS, I got completely lost. Positivity went out the window because I had given up the fight; I just wanted to crawl under a rock and be left alone. However my dad said to me at the beginning of my illness some of the wisest words I have ever heard:

"Son, things will improve; just believe and give it some time."

As time went on, guess what? My dad was right, and after a while, I started to make a little progress in every area of my life. Physically, my symptoms became more manageable, and mentally, my mind started to exercise again. If you close your mind to the possibilities of getting better, I believe that your condition will deteriorate and your symptoms will get worse. This is not a medical opinion, as I am not a doctor; however, enough case studies from cancer patients, MS patients, and those with other conditions show that those who apply a positive approach to their illness can speed up their recovery.

I now believe that you have infinite riches within your reach. To gain them, all you have to do is open your eyes and unlock the treasure chest that each and every person has within their grasp. You can unlock and gain all the things necessary for them to live gloriously, joyously, and abundantly. Unfortunately, many people are closed off to this treasure chest, as they do not know about this infinite intelligence and boundless love within themselves. Whatever you want in life, you can well and truly have.

Let me give you an analogy. A magnetized piece of iron can lift twelve times it is own weight, but if you demagnetize the same piece of iron, it will not lift even a drawing pin. In the very same way, there are two types of people. Those who are magnetized are full of confidence and faith—they know they will succeed and keep on winning. However, many others are demagnetized; they are full of fears and doubts. When an opportunity comes along, they question their own ability to take it, and when they are diagnosed with an illness, they give up and can't get negative thoughts out of their minds. People who are demagnetized find it very difficult to cope with life and unfortunately do not progress very far, and life is more of a struggle. For those of you who feel as if they are in the demagnetized category, you are probably asking yourself, *how can I change and become magnetized?* Well, let me share one of life's very simple but tremendously powerful secrets, one that is worth more than any lottery win. The secret lies in the marvelous miracle working power found in your subconscious mind. This is the last place most people would look for it, which is the reason many don't find it.

Once you learn to contact and release the hidden powers of your subconscious mind, you can bring into your life more power, more wealth, more health, more happiness, and more joy. Most people don't understand that you do not need to acquire this power; you actually possess it already. The problem is most don't know how to use it.

While I was down in the dumps, some lights started to go on in my mind from personal development. For two years, it was total darkness as I had closed off all avenues leading to the subconscious mind. The powers within it were absolutely no good to me. As time passed and the lights started to flicker, I made some of the most important decisions of my life. I decided that I was going to beat the MS, I decided I was going to be a great husband, I decided I was going to have a family, and I decided I was going to be an entrepreneur.

I made all these decisions, and guess what? That's what happened. The biggest decision I made was to open my subconscious mind and release the power within it to give me the tools necessary for me to carry out my plan. Provided you are open minded and receptive, the infinite intelligence within your subconscious mind can reveal to you everything you need to know at any point of time. The person with the open mind and a positive approach to his/her condition will make more progress than the one who has given up. I am true testament to this, and though other factors have contributed to me beating the MS, I can say hand on heart that my positive mental attitude towards my situation supersedes all the other parts of my plan.

If you have a very open mind and great attitude, you will get on the right medication. You will also have the perseverance and commitment to put an exercise regime into play. You will have the perseverance to stick to the right diet plan that will ultimately give you the energy to get through every single day. It is absolutely limitless to what you can achieve if you bring this approach to your daily regime.

A man, sooner or later, discovers that he is the master-gardener of his soul,
the director of his life. James Allen

CHAPTER 9   CHAMPIONS

The message I want to get out to every single person reading this book is to *never give up*. Never give up on your health, never give up on your career, and never give up on your dreams. Life is full of examples of people, both famous and not so famous, who have fought back through all sorts of adversity to conquer.

When I worked out that I really had a chance of beating the MS, I came across people who had fought similar battles and had won their fights. From this, I gained massive encouragement, and as time went on, I continued to study and look for people of this nature. It's incredible that if you can learn to program your mind and put the right plan in place, I believe that you will be close to unstoppable. I listened to so many so called medical experts in the early part of my illness who told me that I wouldn't play football again, wouldn't be able to have a great career, that I couldn't do this and couldn't do that as a result of my MS diagnosis. To be fair, and from a medical point of view, that might be true in many cases. However, I was just not buying into this philosophy and I would encourage you to do the same. You only get one crack at life and my advice is to fight back against your illness; start today and plan for a great life.

Think of this book as a manual to use as you pursue the best in every area of your life. I hope it gives you the inspiration you need to keep putting one foot in front of the other when you grow weary in your journey, and I hope it reminds you over and over again, and in a variety of ways, that you can actually do it—you can get better—but only if you never give up. I would hope that through my experience, you get some strength to rise above the curveballs life throws at you and you come out the other side. I am not an exceptional individual; I am just like you and everyone else with two arms and two legs. In life, I was brought up to treat everyone as equal and I love meeting people and engaging in banter and conversation. However, one ingredient that may separate me from others is that I have developed a tremendous positive attitude, and that's what you need to understand, develop and implement. Attitude is everything, and if you have the right attitude, anything is possible.

One of the reasons that people give up is that they don't always succeed on the first try, and feel like a failure. The reality is that you are only a failure if you give up. If you fail, I advise you to keep going and believing that you will succeed. I now believe that temporary setbacks are part of life and you need to experience these in order to overcome adversity. For those of you out there who never give up, failure is simply the fuel for greater determination and success for the future. As previously discussed, some of the most famous people in history failed, and they refused to give up. I have detailed below some people who have fought back from illness to go on and inspire others to do the same. People like those detailed below continue to be a beacon of hope to us all.

- <u>Montel Williams – MS Champion and media guru - USA</u>

He is the author the New York Times bestselling inspirational memoirs *Climbing Higher* and *Mountain, Get out of My Way*, and the co-author of the New York Times bestseller *Body change*.

Montel also continues to have a very successful television career and is an inspiring entrepreneur. Prior to hosting his own television show, Montel was a special duty intelligence officer in the navy, specializing in cryptology. A graduate of the Naval Academy, he received a number of military awards and citations during his naval career. One of Montel's key beliefs is that "success is determined by what you give back to others," which is why he has worked actively with a variety of charitable organizations throughout the years.

In 1999, Montel announced his diagnosis of MS. He very quickly decided to fight back and to raise awareness and funds for MS research through the Montel Williams Foundation. Through Montel's books and never-say-die attitude, he was one of the first people I came across who inspired me to fight back against my own MS and believe that I could win the battle.

In his book *Climbing Higher* he shares his experience when he had his first consultation with Dr. Olson who was a director of the Department of Molecular Medicine at the Karolinska Institute in Stockholm. Dr. Olson explained to Montel the "seven year rule," or, however you are for seven years will be how you are for the next seven years. If you have experienced any level of worsening or degradation over a seven-year period, it is likely that this will be repeated over the following seven-year period. Dr. Olson advised Montel that this would likely be the rule of thumb until a person reaches a certain age, when it seems to be cancelled.

The knowledge I have gained from Montel through his literature in the past few years has been incredible. I have taken on board many of his tips and advice as they help me fight back. I would greatly encourage you to educate yourself in relation to your MS or your illness, as this will form the nucleus of your plan to fight back. Montel continues to inspire us all that anything is possible.

- Susan Sly – MS Champion and entrepreneur - USA

Susan Sly is a successful entrepreneur, author, speaker, personal empowerment trainer, and MS champion fighter. Susan believes that we all have greatness within us and are truly capable of creating more in our lives. I met Susan in 2010 at a business conference in Las Vegas and was instantly struck by her charisma and amazing attitude, which is ultimately at the root of all her successes—including her fight against MS. She is a truly inspirational leader of the twenty-first century, and a lady who inspires us all to commit to a fruitful, healthy and fulfilling lifestyle.

- Dr Terry Wahls M.D – MS Champion and Clinical Professor of Medicine - USA

In 2003, Terry Wahl's, M.D., was diagnosed with secondary progressive multiple sclerosis and soon became dependent upon a tilt-recline wheelchair. After developing and using the Wahl's Protocol, she is now able to walk through the hospital and commute to work by bicycle. She now uses intensive directed nutrition in her primary care and traumatic brain injury clinics. Dr. Wahls is the lead scientist in a clinical trial testing her protocol in others with progressive MS. Through her plan that got her back to good health, and her never-give-up attitude, she is now inspiring others to do the same. A truly inspirational women and MS champion Fighter.

- Mark Pollock – Inspirational fighter and adventure athlete - Northern Ireland

Unbroken by the loss of his sight at twenty-two years of age and a paralyzing fall thirteen years later, Mark Pollock has made surviving catastrophic change an art form and continues to inspire audiences worldwide.

For the last decade, the blind adventure athlete has competed in the harshest environments on the planet. He survived sub-zero Antarctic temperatures as he raced to the South Pole. He suffered in scorching heat, running six marathons in the Gobi Desert in one week. He has run a marathon at The North Pole, raced through the desert lowlands of the Syrian African Rift Valley to the Dead Sea and competed at high-altitude in the Everest Marathon.

Mark has competed against professional explorers like Sir Ranulph Fiennes, Olympic gold medalists and Special Forces personnel—all able-bodied athletes—and he has done so in a world of total darkness.

After a life-threatening fall in 2011, Mark is now competing against his spinal cord injury. Paralyzed from the waist down, Mark's next adventure race is against his own body, challenging conventional wisdom that there is no way out this time.

Mark is a living example to all of us that with the right attitude and application you can fight against adversity, no matter what, and win the battle. He is a true warrior and inspiration to us all. I challenge anyone to read Mark's story and fail to be inspired—it is impossible not to be.

- Helen Keller – The ultimate overcomer - USA

One of the best-known overcomers in American history is a lady by the name of Helen Keller. She profusely refused to allow the blindness of her eyes and deafness of her ears to keep her from enjoying her life, hitting her goals, and making a significant contribution to society.

Up to nineteen months, Helen's life was pretty normal, but this all changed when she became very sick with what was then termed a brain fever. The disease left her severely handicapped and without the ability of sight and hearing. Her parents took her to see Alexander Graham Bell, the famous inventor of the telephone, who was also a specialist teacher of the deaf and helped those with hearing difficulties. He referred Helen to the Boston Perkins School for the Blind. The school provided Helen with a supervisor by the name of Ann Sullivan whom Helen referred to as Teacher until Sullivan's death. As a young child, Helen struggled with her handicaps and often became angry and frustrated. However, over time her teacher continued to support and assist her eventually teaching her to read, write, and communicate effectively, despite the fact she was born blind and deaf.

As a young child, Helen had made her mind up that she wanted to go to college, and after studying hard, she was accepted to Radcliff College, the women's school associated with Harvard University. Four years later, she had mastered several languages and graduated with honours. In college, Helen embarked on a writing career, which lasted over fifty years and included books, newspapers, articles, and magazine pieces. Her first book was published in 1903 and finely found its way into print in more than fifty languages. Before her death in 1968, Helen had received many awards and an honorary degree in recognition of her work and inspiring attitude with how she very gracefully led her life. One of the reasons Helen fought and beat adversity was that her teacher, Ann Sullivan, never gave up on her and helped her achieve her goals.

I encourage you to never give up on yourself; with the right attitude, you can achieve fulfilment. I hope this story also encourages you to inspire others to persevere though their own difficulties and overcome their challenges, just like you have done yourself.

The above champions are all people who have developed and applied an unbreakable attitude to life and an incredible mindset in how to cope, manage, and ultimately fight against all the odds that were stacked against them.

I can relate to each of these people, as in the very early days of my MS diagnosis, I was really struggling to see any light at the end of the tunnel. However, there is always light at the end of the tunnel, and in fact, I have yet to drive into a tunnel and not come out the other end to see the light. Think about that one!

We human beings tend to give up when things don't seem to go our way. The belief that life will simply roll over, give in to our demands, and allow us to achieve our goals is unrealistic. The truth is that life is neither for nor against us. No, life is simply just the natural process of existence. What we have to understand is that the power to determine the direction our life takes is not decided by life itself, but rather by us. We hold the power, regardless of the challenges we may face. Therefore, our power rests in how we handle our daily interactions within the context of life. These interactions are what determine our ability to overcome what we may perceive as insurmountable odds. Therefore, we must learn not to blame life itself for our successes or failures. Instead, when faced with challenges, we must simply stand our ground and work smarter with a never-give-up attitude firmly in place.

Think of the following and see if you agree. Life is like a blank piece of paper. As that paper exists, so do we. However, just like that paper is blank, so too is our life until we create something out of it. Until that piece of paper is written on, there is no story, no direction, no purpose, but there is endless possibility (positive or negative—you determine that by the story you write). However, interesting things begin to happen as soon as we begin to write on that piece of paper. A story starts to emerge, a direction begins to tug at us, a purpose starts to form, and meaning that gives life to passion sets in.

The same occurs when we choose to engage life. However, this engagement does not come without pitfalls. You will find in many classic Disney stories such as that of Snow White, Pinocchio, and Cinderella that the main characters often have to overcome seemingly insurmountable pitfalls and challenges in order to achieve their dreams. My point is that we need to reinforce in our children from a young age that never giving up is essential to achieving our dreams, much like our childhood literary heroes.

Therefore, regardless of the pitfalls or the challenges you may encounter in life, know that you get the final say in writing and living your life's story. With all of this in mind, I ask the question, what are you writing on your blank piece of paper called life? Are you utilizing the words and thought processes of a quitter—one who buckles to the challenges of life that we all face? Or, are you uti-

CONOR DEVINE

lizing the words and thought processes of a winner—one who never gives up in pursuit of his/her vision?

I implore you to take on the role of the winner, and not to quit in the face of adversity. Do not succumb to life's challenges, and never stop creating and working on making your life's vision a reality. Remember, everyone has challenges to overcome. Life is full of them, but be passionate about your dreams and continue to push forward, even when it seems most difficult.

After I had been down in the dumps for some time, some lights started to go on in my mind as I strove for personal development. For two years, it seemed as though I had lived in total darkness. I had closed off all avenues leading to the subconscious mind. The powers within it were absolutely no good to me, as my mental health was not in great order. As time passed and the lights started to flicker, through some guidance I started to make decisions that were the most important decisions I have ever had to make. I decided that I was going to beat the MS; I decided I was going to be a great husband; I decided I was going to have a family; I decided I was going to be an entrepreneur.

I made all these decisions and that's exactly what happened. The biggest decision I made was to open my subconscious mind and release the power within it to give me the tools necessary for me to carry out my plan. Provided you are open minded and receptive, the infinite intelligence within your subconscious mind can reveal to you everything you need to know at any point in your life.

I meet people every day and many do not know I have MS. When I tell them, they cannot believe it at all because I look so well. Their next reaction seems to be one of a little pity, as it's very sad that one so young should have to deal with this condition. Most times when I see people going down this route—taking the road of pitying me—I am looking back at them thinking, *hi pal, I'm way fitter, stronger, and mentally healthier than you are, so thanks for your concern, but I'm terrific.*

The reason I can think this way is because I have a tremendous attitude, and as you now know, *Attitude is Everything.*

If you have a bad attitude, you will have a mediocre life at best, as you won't get to meet great people, you will likely not succeed at your work, if you get sick you won't have the skill set required to help you fight it, and the list goes on and on. If you have the right attitude, then you can achieve anything you want.

When I started thinking about writing this book, I mentioned it to a few people, and some laughed and said, "You'll never write a book." Maybe people thought rightly or wrongly that I wasn't the book writing type and you know what, maybe they are right. However, I have written my book and I am really chuffed that I have this opportunity to share my story with people from all corners of the world. I am excited by the fact that there are people reading this book from the USA, Australia, Ireland, the UK, and other parts of Europe. Five years ago, I never would have thought this was possible, not in my wildest dreams, but I've done it.

I am a living example of someone who is beating MS every single day, and I am now living a very privileged life on all fronts. Four years ago I thought this was impossible. Well, it is possible, as I am now a young, gregarious thirty-five-year-old with what I believe to have the world at my feet. I have more goals now than ever, and I believe that I will hit every one of them. It's a great way to live your life, and it's a great way to be and feel. Of course I have bad days; who doesn't? But that's normal. The next morning I get up and say to myself, "You know what, I am going to try harder today than I did yesterday."

I now know what it feels like to hit a wall, to be wiped out, to be diagnosed with a potentially devastating illness at such a young age. However, I would not change any of it, as I now believe that my MS diagnosis has changed me as a person for the better, and my life as a result of my diagnosis is fantastic. I know that sounds pretty weird, but it's the truth.

Whatever your challenges are—maybe its obesity, cancer, alcoholism, mental health issues, whatever the case maybe—get some help, and when you begin to get a clearer picture of the future, start putting the ingredients in place to develop a bullet-proof attitude. If you do this, you will reap the benefits.

I would like to thank you very much for taking the time to read my book. I hope you put into practice some of the ingredients I have brought into my life that have helped me to succeed.

I would like to finally share a mindset with you that you need to read at least a dozen times before you realize how powerful the words actually are. Roy Keane, the very famous ex Manchester United footballer and subsequent manager, used to have this on the wall of the changing rooms so the players could read it before they took the field. I now have this hanging very proudly in my own home, and I read it every day. I truly believe it is extremely powerful and very relevant to survive in this mad world we all live in. I hope you enjoy it.

If you think you are beaten,
You are.
If you think you dare not,
You don't.

If you'd like to win
But you think you can't,
It is almost certain you won't.
Life's battles don't always go to
The stronger or faster man,
But sooner or later the man who
Wins is the man who thinks he can!

From "The Man Who Thinks He Can"
By Walter D. Wintle

On Sunday 4th November 2012, I ran my second marathon in Central park New York City, along with twenty thousand other enthusiastic runners, from all corners of the globe. I recorded a new personal best of 3 hours 59 minutes, which was an incredible feeling of satisfaction and achievement. Although the official marathon was cancelled due to hurricane "Sandy", I hadn't trained for the past six months, travelled to the USA to sit back and not smash my goal and complete my challenge. I got my medal and more importantly I proved to myself and my body that I am in control and that I am beating MS. My attitude prepared me for this challenge and got me through it in the end, and what a euphoric feeling it is to achieve something medically you are not really expected to be doing.

Well I did it and I just hope that in some small way, you can develop your own attitude and platform that will allow you to achieve and smash your own goals.

I am currently writing my personal, business and health goals for 2013 and I truly intend to achieve every one of them. I look forward to the challenges life will continue to throw at me, safe in the knowledge that no matter how difficult they may be, I am capable of winning the battles and achieving fulfillment.

I really hope you enjoyed my story and I would invite you all to visit my MS Awareness website at www.conordevine.com

Take care everyone and remember *ATTITUDE IS EVERYTHING*

Printed in Great Britain
by Amazon.co.uk, Ltd.,
Marston Gate.